THE ·TRAINS· WE LOVED

The Bristolian

The year is 1959 and in July Warship diesel-hydraulics will take over from steam power on the Bristolian—but for now steam is king. Bath Road 'Castle' No 5078 Beaufort *is ready for a fast run up to Paddington. A west to north train awaits departure in charge of a London Midland 'Patriot' No 45509* The Derbyshire Yeomanry *while in the centre road a local Pannier tank idles between duties. The magnificent roof of Bristol Temple Meads still remains and*

has in fact been restored in recent years although this particular view has been ruined by the appearance of an ugly Royal Mail bridge at the London end of the platforms. Train-spotters were an ever-present feature at stations large and small and the artist has included two of the breed who are noting down their latest 'cops'. Their inclusion also serves to add scale and a certain majesty to the locomotives and the imposing surroundings. Station pigeons complete the scene.

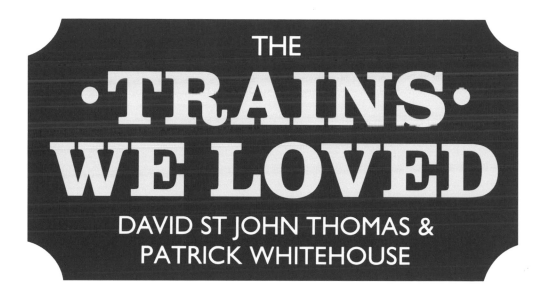

THE ·TRAINS· WE LOVED

DAVID ST JOHN THOMAS & PATRICK WHITEHOUSE

With 32 paintings
by PHILIP HAWKINS

David & Charles

ACKNOWLEDGEMENTS

Most of the text is by David St John Thomas and much of it based on his personal memories of extensive travel during his early years as a journalist. Patrick Whitehouse had, however, sketched out four chapters (his very last writing) before his sad death in June 1993. Early Memories of Two Lines to New Street and To Beyond Middleton Top are based on favourite reminiscences, while Joint Ventures is the retelling of a vivid tale of years ago. The chapter on Ireland is a compilation of recollections of many happy visits. On one such journey to the Tralee & Dingle Patrick met John Powell, who for the last decade has been an active member of the team supporting the two authors. Alas John also died in 1993, and before preparing his usual contribution to the joint titles. He had however helped in the planning of this book designed to evoke the many and varied aspects of travel at the end of the steam era. One of the most compelling attractions in those days was the Trent Valley. While most young Midland enthusiasts went to Tamworth, Chris Jones shows why other locations also had their devotees. The Millbrook House team who helped see the project through on this occasion were John Edgington, David Johnson and John Smart. They were responsible for the black and white illustrations and their captions.

The colour, however, is uniquely the work of a single artist, the chairman of the Guild of Railway Artists, Philip Hawkins. His knowledge and enthusiasm, as some of the captions make clear, exactly dovetails with that of the authors. This is the first time a collection of his work has appeared in a book, and we hope and expect it will create much interest. For those who might like to secure a larger quality print, nine of the subjects included are the subject of Quicksilver Publishing prints (details from The Sidings, 52 Teignmouth Road, Teignmouth, TQ14 8AS; tel (0626) 773288).

The black and white photographs are gratefully acknowledged as follows:

P.M. Alexander/Millbrook House Collection (17 lower, 18, 20, 23, 26, 33, 39, 41, 52, 56 both, 57, 60, 61, 82, 84, 95 upper, 96, 113 both, 160, 161, 182 both, 184, 185 upper, 186 lower); H. Ballantyne (25, 90, 123, 127); H.C. Casserley (149); K. Cooper (169, 170, 171); T.J. Edgington (83, 101, 132); W.L. Good (45); P.W. Gray (29 lower, 114); G.F. Heiron (8); R.G. Jarvis (177); D.A. Johnson (13, 27, 71, 79, 85, 87, 124, 126, 136, 163, 185 lower, 186 upper); C. Jones Collection (73 upper, 118, 122, 179); J.D. Mills (81); C.F.H. Oldham (17 upper, 30); J. Robertson/Colour Rail (112, 143); W.J. Probert (117, 129, 130), E. Treacy/Millbrook House Collection (12, 19, 21, 22, 65, 67, 68, 73 lower, 74, 77, 78, 80, 89, 93, 95 lower, 104, 108, 125, 131 lower, 133, 138, 144, 145, 148, 153, 180, 183); E.R. Wethersett (181); P.B. Whitehouse (28, 29 upper, 44 both, 46, 47, 119, 121, 131 upper, 134, 142, 164, 166, 167, 168, 172, 175 both, 176, 178 both); and Millbrook House Collection (43, 49, 97, 139, 141, 165).

A DAVID & CHARLES BOOK

Hardback edition first published 1994
Paperback edition published 2002

Distributed in North America
by F&W Publications, Inc.

ISBN 0 7153 1383 5

Printed in China by
Hong Kong Graphics & Printing Ltd.
for David & Charles
Brunel House   Newton Abbot   Devon

Page six, top King on the Cambrian

Today the bridge over Hatton bank plays host to hoards of camera-toting enthusiasts who flock to watch steam specials, but until the end of steam on BR it was usually deserted. The year is 1960 and No 6015 King Richard III is exerting maximum effort in heaving the down Cambrian coast express up the 1 in 110 Warwickshire gradient. The distinct change in colour of the bricks betrays the fact that, during the fifties, it partially collapsed and was repaired with brand new bricks. The King displays the decorative version of the headboard which Stafford Road and Old Oak Common seemed to prefer at this time. 6015 would be replaced at Wolverhampton or, in later years, Shrewsbury where invariably a Manor would take over for the remainder of the journey to the Cambrian coast.

CONTENTS

1 The Trains We Loved   9
2 On Board   19
3 Western   25
4 Winter   32
5 School Outings   38
6 Early Memories of Two Lines to New Street   42
7 Southern   53
8 Stations   64
9 Village Stop   75
10 London Midland   77
11 Spring   84
12 Joint Ventures   88
13 Central Figure   91
14 Eastern   93
15 Paddington–St Ives   105
16 Summer   115
17 Trent Valley in the Fifties   122
18 North Eastern   129
19 Eventide   135
20 Eating en Route   138
21 Scottish   142
22 Autumn   157
23 To Beyond Middleton Top   164
24 Ireland   168
25 Another Route   179
26 Inverness–Euston   187
   Index   191

Opposite below **On Time**

In sharp contrast to the 'competition' across the city centre, Birmingham Snow Hill was a bright and cheery place and remarkably so when one considers how busy it was. The year is 1947, the last before nationalisation, and a King No 6008 King James II runs into platform 7, well on time, with the midday service to London Paddington. Snow Hill became extremely busy in the early sixties when many London trains were transferred from New Street to ease traffic during the London Midland electrification. It was a bitter blow to many 'brummies' when complete closure came in 1971. A new, albeit smaller and far less grand station, was opened on the site in 1988. The painting was commissioned in 1985 by the Birmingham Post & Mail Ltd to commemorate the 150th anniversary of the Great Western Railway.

Above **Birmingham New Street**

The Midland Railway side of New Street retained its overall roof until the entire complex was rebuilt in 1964. It afforded the receptive onlooker wonderfully evocative light patterns as sunlight forced a way through the smoke, steam and general grime. A Fowler 'Patriot' 4–6–0 No 45506 The Royal Pioneer Corps is standing at platform 7 with a train from its home town of Bristol and will be going onto Sheffield, York or Newcastle. For a few years in the late fifties, and until 1962, Bristol Barrow Road shed had three 'Patriots' on its allocation, Nos 45504/6/19. They were among the artist's favourite locomotives and sadness was inevitable when the last unrebuilt examples were withdrawn from service in 1962.

1
THE TRAINS WE LOVED

MORE people talk fondly about their railway than any other recollections, and more memorabilia from train travel and spotting has been preserved than for any other hobby. This unashamedly nostalgic book celebrates the trains we loved—those of our childhood and those that our parents perhaps told us about in vivid detail. It takes its name from one of the most famous books ever produced for railway enthusiasts, written by Hamilton Ellis at the end of World War II and published in 1947 while Britain's railways were still privately owned. But while Hamilton Ellis looked back to what he considered were the Great Days before the numerous highly-individual railways were grouped into four in 1923, our period of fond memory is that on either side of nationalisation, again within living memory for many—and certainly within the memory of our parents. Our aim as authors is to recapture the readers' yesterdays and unless you smell and hear the trains we describe and illustrate as well as recall their individual character and performance we shall have failed in our task.

We do, however, have some claim to success: well over a quarter of a million copies of the other twelve volumes under our joint authorship have been sold, and indeed much is owed to reader participation in providing material. Sadly, this was to be the last work on which we worked together: Patrick Whitehouse, my partner, died shortly after writing his first contributions to the following pages. Any partnership that lasts for a dozen major titles was clearly solidly based, and his companionship, encouragement and constructive criticism are much missed. The completion of this book, which was conceived appropriately enough on a stroll along the Sea Wall from Teignmouth to near the entrance to Parson's Tunnel, is in large measure a tribute to Patrick who in words and pictures, and in his major contribution to the railway preservation movement, did so much to keep alive the memories of the trains we loved.

Occasionally I have had to ask myself if we were mad in having such affection for them, and also question whether our period straddling but mainly after World War II actually included the Great Days. In presenting the picture as truthfully as possible, it has been necessary to point out shortcomings like the lousy station work on my own favourite Western Region. Yet not only were these the trains we had, and which took us on just about every important journey in our life, but many of us feel extremely fortunate to have experienced such a rich rail age.

If there was not quite the variety of pre-Grouping locomotive types and livery, it was nearly a decade after nationalisation before the proportion of the total locomotive stock that was of pre-Grouping origin was reduced to a third. Historic relics abounded, some systems being veritable steam

Brand new BR Britannia class 4–6–2 No 70004 William Shakespeare *stands at Stewarts Lane shed, Battersea suitably adorned for working the Golden Arrow, 11am Victoria to Dover Marine.* William Shakespeare *was on display at the Festival of Britain exhibition on the South Bank (at the end of Hungerford Bridge) in 1951 and is seen here still carrying the special exhibition finish.*

Overleaf The Midlander
When the artist was growing up in Birmingham during the fifties, The Midlander became a familiar friend as it passed along the embankment at the back of his home in Winson Green. Stanier Jubilee 4–6–0s were the regular motive power and were allocated to Bushbury shed in Wolverhampton. No 45688 Polyphemus was one of the regulars and is seen here running into platform 6 at Birmingham New Street at the end of a two hour run from Euston in the mid-fifties. In the background at platform 3, a Fowler 2–6–4 tank is waiting to leave with a local train, perhaps for Lichfield, while a Black 5 has its thirst quenched at platform 1. The Rotunda now dominates the centre background. The distinctive Worcester Street buildings above the signal box disappeared during the rebuilding in 1964. With a generous helping of imagination it is just possible to picture the scene today—if one can ignore the plethora of overhead catenary equipment.

Philip D. Hawkins

Above **New Street 1957**
On summer Saturdays in the fifties, huge numbers of day-trippers and holidaymakers invaded stations throughout the country to catch excursion trains to the seaside. Here, at Birmingham New Street, the artist has caught the holiday mood with trains standing at platforms 9 and 10 bound for the West Country. The locomotives are Patriot No 45509 The Derbyshire Yeomanry *and Jubilee No 45682* Trafalgar. *The grand roof was, by this stage, rather dilapidated and if anything looks more imposing than it actually was. The typical British holidaymakers' uniform of coats and macs is noticeable and the 'cheap day' poster is a reminder of pre-decimalisation days.*

Opposite above **Rush Hour at Rubery**
The motive power on view here is a reminder that the Longbridge to Halesowen line in the West Midlands was a joint Midland and Great Western Railway venture. A Tyseley-based Pannier tank No 7402 is running through Rubery station, watched intently by a member of the local canine population, with a workman's train for the Austin car factory at Longbridge. Waiting in the loop with a freight working is an ex-Midland railway 2F 0–6–0. Because of severe weight restrictions over Dowery Dell viaduct, only locomotives with a light axle loading were allowed.

4
WINTER

WINTER, of course began as the Christmas traffic was reaching its crescendo and the darkest days were often doing their worst. Most railwaymen took a keen interest in the seasonal traffic, passenger and freight. Nobody's Christmas could happen without their efforts.

Except in years of great fogs, when sometimes trains were so badly delayed that animals had to be slaughtered en route, most livestock had been safely delivered to Smithfield and other markets by 21 December and the only turkeys in transit were those belonging to individual travellers, many to be given as presents, a few to stationmasters and leading porters. Parcels and mail were however still in full flow. These last few days before Christmas were indeed the most difficult of all, mountains of mail delaying the departures of numerous passenger trains while extra parcels and perishables for ever seemed to be on the block.

While many of the famous named trains and also the prime businessmen's trains went their way without Post Office hindrance, delays to those that took all the mail waiting for them were often prodigious. Add bad weather, and cross-country and especially overnight services were sometimes reported so many hundred minutes late that it was hard work to convert it to hours and minutes. Yet it was nearly all good-humoured, with passengers, realising they would be stuck for twenty minutes here and there, raiding refreshment rooms and moving closer to each other to engage in life-revealing conversations. Station inspectors treated onlookers and participants in the loading of mail with equal joviality. In those days there was much more parcel post, and it nearly all went by train. Many specials were run. At Birmingham, for example, the goods shed at Monument Lane was cleared of ordinary traffic and the Post Office took over from 9 or 10 December until Christmas Eve.

Especially before and during World War II, a driver or fireman might descend from his footplate to help stow bags into a leading van. There being much less business (and no 'junk') mail in those days, the Christmas rush was proportionately greater than now. The Travelling Post Offices were of course abandoned, being totally unable to cope and their staff (along with the extra Christmas Post Office staff wearing their own clothes but with an official PO band around the right arm) helped build and demolish heaps of mail bags, often eight or nine feet high on main platforms.

Passenger and goods parcels offices were likewise overwhelmed, every category of their business being busier than usual, but the ultimate pressure was the PLA (Passengers' Luggage in Advance) of children returning from boarding school along with boxes and crates of all shapes and sizes conveying family Christmas presents. Christmas did not start early in those

days; apart from livestock it nearly all happened in the last fortnight. Often parcels offices literally overflowed, a waiting room sometimes being taken over at least for night storage or in country areas crates and boxes being left in the open. An unexpected frost could take its toll, but then slow-moving goods trains offering a much more affordable parcels rate were of course unheated. A visit to one of the large goods stations gave you the very smell of Christmas, and you would see large branches of holly strategically placed for decoration till they were collected and where pieces of mistletoe had been surreptitiously snipped off. Considering the low wages and great visual temptation of just about every seasonal luxury going, from crates of fine port to turkeys and other birds with a label round their neck, the lack of pilferage was a tribute to the railwayman's profession.

The last two working days before Christmas saw the emphasis change to passengers, many of whom were given faster journeys at the last moment than those who thought they would beat the rush but ran into that for mail.

An early member of the GW Hall class 4–6–0 No 4912 Berrington Hall *runs along what looks like newly laid flat-bottom rail track near Dauntsey with the 9.35am Weymouth to Swindon ordinary passenger service on 30 November 1952. The leading vans will probably have been attached at Chippenham carrying traffic from Harris's sausage factory at Calne.*

more interested pacing the platform listening to the bells in the signal box at its end, or at least emerging into the cold when the signals changed. Surely one of the excitements of travelling by train was that you did not have a visual display of how late your service would be. Expectantly you might hear the approaching steam locomotive, first questioning its slackness but quickly realising that here was another freight whose load would probably be mainly coal going to be burnt in all manner of grates to help keep people warm.

A journey by scantily-patronised express on a crisp, clear day in midwinter was surely travelling at its most luxurious and memorable. Oh, that steam heat! Today we have to pay to enjoy it; once it was free to all who knew how to soak it in. Even when stationary, winter trains were never silent, the hiss of escaping steam that enveloped joining passengers having an almost musical quality. Each compartment had its steam-heating control knob or handle, usually high up on the partition above the seats (or adjacent to the window); sometimes each side had its separate control. The heat released from the broad pipe under the seat was never dry or oppressive. It might send you to sleep as it worked its magic in every pore, but there was no risk of headache or hangover. Steam heat: the very words spell nostalgic magic!

Snow. Falling snow as evil as the thickest fog, prohibiting many shunting movements. Windblown snow getting between the point blades and human beings, with only a brazier to prevent them freezing, doing what point heaters are supposed to do today. Treacherous blizzards closing Highland passes; forcing signalmen to walk instead of cycle between the separate ground frames at the end of the station; occasionally stopping trains in deep drifts, the passengers kept warm by the steam engine until the rescue party broke through. But more often snow the railway's friend, not enough to disrupt it seriously but causing chaos on the roads. Again imagine the scene, this time at a country station.

Normally only five passengers now get the morning service into town and that despite a rapid growth in population. Most of the locals have changed to the bus which starts from the village square, while the incomers drive to their town jobs. Today however thirty to forty pick their way down the footpath across the fields to the station, a few more by the road whose virgin snow has yet to be disturbed by motor wheels. The stationmaster is ready for them. Normally down passengers use the fire in the up waiting room, but this morning the expectant stationmaster has ordered his sole porter (junior at that) to light the fire in the down one, and a nice glow it gives. One and two at a time, the passengers, some of whom have always intended to patronise the train and now feel good about doing so, waddle up to the booking office window and buy their cheap day tickets; they are told 'she' will be about fifteen minutes late.

As the tank engine comes round the curve giving a warning toot the stationmaster leaves the junior in charge of the office to sell tickets to any latecomers and goes over to exercise his skills as social host. If he hopes to secure regular travellers through his efforts, he will be disappointed. Yet in a sense they pay off, for several of the once-in-five-years passengers swear a kind of oath of allegiance to the railway—'absolutely essential for bad weather like this'—and will be supportive in any discussion about its future, in some cases for the next quarter of a century until it is closed.

A typical handbill, measuring 6¼" × 10" produced to advertise forthcoming excursion facilities such as this one to a First Division football match at Roker Park, Sunderland.

One of the major purposes of the trains we loved was of course to show us our own country and, since snow made a greater visual impact than any other winter condition, winter journeys were often especially fascinating… by day and by night when there was a full moon and you could expect to see a fox stealthily following the hedge round a field's edge. We were frequently amazed by how much more or less snow had fallen on districts close together, and loved the softening impact of the white blanket on the usually severe industrial landscapes through which trains tended to enter large towns. Often a friend in the countryside but enemy in town, the railway now universally disappeared into the scenery, and at marshalling yards and goods depots you could instantly tell which tracks had been used and which not.

Snow and ice were just two interrupters of the normal winter routine. A particularly exciting one was football specials. Excursion offices and station-masters watched with bated breath to see who would play who and what traffic opportunities that offered. Except where there was heavy commuter traffic (not of course yet described by that name), many stations were used by more special-event than ordinary passengers. In addition to the football there was racing, speedway, boxing, hunting… anything people could be persuaded they needed to go and see personally. The well-to-do still occasionally went by train, the groom riding in the horse box, to distant hunts. Enginemen were asked to keep a sharp look out for hunts in full cry. Special fares were provided for the pantomime until mid-January. Educational specials to places like Windsor and York started up in earnest in the last few weeks of the spring term.

And when passengers came off the last service from the nearest city on a Saturday night, some reeking of fish and chips, and the late-turn porter or signalman went round turning the gas lamps off, there was merriment emphasising that for many social life depended on there being a convenient train. What was next week's film?

But there is one last image of late winter: the evening expresses going to a resort with in almost every compartment a newly-married couple alone. These were the days when the tax system encouraged wedlock before the end of the financial year, and since not every couple could be accommodated on the very last Saturdays the marriage business was on a serious scale even by the beginning of March. In some resorts there were hotels totally devoted to honeymooners before the season proper started, and there we see the Devonian toward the end of its journey from Bradford to Paignton. On other nights there are many empty compartments, but tonight being Saturday the honeymooners are out in force and it is almost as though the number of couples allowed on board has been calculated by the number of compartments. There they are, nestling into each other with what hopes and fears we can only guess, over fifty couples each in seclusion. Who would be a ticket collector on this train?

before swinging off the Wolverhampton main line with a slowing at Harborne Junction box to take the staff. Then the regulator opens for the climb up over the canal, through now closed Icknield Port Road station and so over 1 in 66 to the summit at Hagley Road. The North Western engine emits a throaty roar as it tackles the bank, cinders cascading onto the coach roofs and the grassy cutting sides. One soon learns, painfully, not to put one's head out of the window. Five and a half minutes from Monument Lane and nine and a half minutes from New Street comes the one passing place, Rotton Park Road station, an island platform with the electric train staff apparatus in the porters' room, levers for points and signals on the platform. Just prior to this is the triangle of tracks for Mitchells & Butlers brewery, another piece of excitement for the firm has a couple of shunters of its own including an ancient Aveling & Porter flywheel drive machine named *John Barleycorn*. Rotton Park Road serves this main artery at one end and the busy City Road at the other. It is another good source of passengers as the buses have not yet taken a hold. To help matters, for a few trains this is the first stop.

Up once more, still at 1 in 66 to the single platform Hagley Road station with its small goods yard for coal merchants serving the large houses in the area. This is *much* posher than Harborne and home to most of the line's first-class passengers: the station even boasts a ladies' waiting room. Hagley Road is reached by a tarmac ramp with bushes on either side, the wide carriageway is lined with trees. In the centre of the road are the 3ft 6in gauge tracks of Birmingham Corporation Tramways, the railway's enemy. Their replacement by buses in 1930 will spell death to the branch passenger services.

From Hagley Road, it is downhill again at 1 in 66 first through a deep cutting, then twisting along an embankment once past the bridge under gentrified Woodbourne Road and looking down on acres of allotments, more plebeian than those near to Somerset Road station. Over the high arched bridge at Park Hill Road, a slowing on the curve past the tall home signal, the dropping of the staff and crawl into Harborne station. All change. Carriage doors open and are slammed back, tickets collected at the double doors and the walk home begins.

The child's fare from Harborne to New Street is three ha'pence return, half the price of the No 4 bus service which is certainly more convenient and which will, in a short time, conquer. The ideal time to get to the station is just before 12.30pm as this allows a look at the returning lunch time trains at 12.38pm, 1.45pm and 2.08pm before a wait for the arrival of the tender engine turn which forms the 2.59pm out. This arrives at 2.26pm and Doreen is there to ask if it is possible for her charge to have a ride round. The enginemen are unable to avoid her charms and it is arranged—the first footplate trip ever. This train is rarely full so it is an empty compartment with button back seats, a couple of thumps (severely discouraged) producing a dusty cloud. The train crawls up to Hagley Road, stops, drops down to Rotton Park, stops again and once more at the disused Icknield Port Road platform where there is a double arm home and distant signal guarding the home at the canal curve before Harborne Junction. This stop almost a normal procedure (as the timetable slot on to the main line is short and their trains are *never* held) is another nail in the coffin of the branch. Occasionally

the delay is so bad that passengers who have to be back at work jump over the fence and get a tram into town. Eventually the home arm falls and the Cauliflower drops down over the junction to Monument Lane platform, where there is yet another delay while tickets are collected, as New Street is an open station. Off past the shed and down through the tunnel into No 2 platform at New Street where time has been allowed in the working timetable for a prompt departure. The fireman puts the slacker hose into his bucket on the footplate and has a swill down getting ready for the next climb up Gravelly Hill bank and on to Sutton Coldfield, Four Oaks and Lichfield City. It is start stop start stop all day.

Harborne station in LNWR days c1908. A train from New Street is entering hauled by a Webb 2-4-2 tank. The stock is a four-coach 'Inter-District Set' of 50ft cove roof vehicles. The original box, seen here, was replaced soon after the photograph was taken.

49

Lyme Regis Bound

During BR days, and until 1961, the Lyme Regis branch attracted enthusiasts from far and wide because of its ancient motive power in the shape of three aged Adams radial tanks. They proved to be the only engines which were ideally suited to working this unusually difficult and twisting seven mile route which left the ex-London & South Western main line at Axminster. The painting features one of these old-timers No 30583 wearing BR lined black livery, which suited it well. This particular engine has now been preserved for more than thirty years on the Bluebell Railway.

Halwill Junction

For many years, Dugald Drummond's T9s—known by all and sundry as Greyhounds—were associated with the Southern's North Devon and Cornwall lines. The Withered Arm, as the lines west of Exeter were known, was leisurely to say the least. That most of it survived until the sixties surprised many observers. Halwill Junction would burst into life with simultaneous arrivals and then lapse once again into suspended animation. Time seems to stand still after the arrival of No 30711 with a mixed train for Okehampton in the fifties. The station, actually called 'Halwill for Beaworthy', was some two miles from the village of Halwill, but a new village that grew up around the station was called Halwill Junction—and retains the name long after the last trains called in the 1960s.

7
SOUTHERN

THE red carpet has been laid out in a pretty matter-of-fact kind of manner, and indeed it is the third time this week the gang has been responsible for preparing a VIP welcome. Electric trains come and go, some of them (to the expert eye) in fact steam carriages of yesteryear placed on new chassis and provided with electric power: progress with economy. Most are running punctually, but when one arrives six minutes later its driver jumps out and runs the length of its twelve carriages to help catch up time. He is in his front compartment ready for the return, his guard has green flag in hand, eleven hundred people have alighted, a hundred and fifty or so get on, all doors have been closed, and the signal has gone green... all in five minutes. Now that is how a railway should be run.

The passengers (who have been delayed waiting for the late train two platforms away) are perhaps as curious as to what locomotive will bring in the VIP special as to his or her identity. Kings and queens and of course film stars excite interest, but prime ministers of fragments of Empire or mini-Middle East countries attract little attention as virtually nobody has heard of them or recognises them. It is red carpet by protocol, and the officials waiting for today's arrival are obviously second class since nobody recognises them either. Now the special arrives, consisting mainly of Pullman cars. It is in fact double headed, by two venerable 4–4–0 tender locomotives of the T9 class, the lovely 'Greyhounds'.

Still the electrics come and go, disgorging in an orderly manner many of London's best-heeled workers who cross the gracefully-curved concourse with dignity. But there is plenty of steam, too. Holidaymakers eagerly board a train for the South West; 'Summer Comes Early to the Southern' boasts a poster. And now another arriving train—also mainly Pullmans and obviously from a ship at Southampton—attracts more attention; photographers and onlookers jostle for position as an under-clad yet overdressed American lady, clearly out of the movies, poses as she alights and re-alights, irritating businessmen waiting behind who are no doubt equally rich if less famous. And still the electrics come and go. There is no prize for guessing that the station is Waterloo, jewel among the Southern's London termini, doubling up as international gateway to London and the place where tens of thousands of suburban folk arrive for their day's work... also starting point for West Country and many other holidays. The scene could equally well be in the 1930s or 1950s, and for those of us who enjoyed it after nationalisation—especially after Southern stock regained its green with amazing alacrity—therein lay the magic. Things did not have to be new to be good.

The Southern was, of course, the smallest of the

An ancient LB&SCR 'Terrier' 0–6–0T leaves the modern concrete of Havant station with the 12.35pm Hayling Island service, comprising a newly repainted LSWR brake composite, on 4 March 1950. It was the light axle loading of the 'Terriers' which allowed them to operate over the wooden Langston viaduct. BR No 32661 had an excellent record of service; built in 1875, it was not withdrawn until 1963, the year the Hayling Island branch was closed.

Overleaf Evercreech Junction
This station really came to life on summer Saturdays, as indeed did the Somerset & Dorset in general, particularly during the fifties. Holidays with pay for all came ahead of mass car ownership, but this quickly followed and was the main reason for the line's eventual demise in 1966. Thanks to the marvellous photographs and wonderfully evocative ciné film taken by the late Ivo Peters, the delights of the S&D are widely known and loved. The line's Derby-built 2–8–0s were fascinating engines, quite unlike anything else. The fact that they were regularly employed on passenger duties only added to their appeal. The artist has chosen to feature one of the preserved members of the class: No 53808, which has the assistance of one of the lines 4–4–0s No 40700. Approaching with a train-load of returning holidaymakers is a Southern Region unrebuilt West Country Pacific No 34043 Combe Martin.

Philip D. Hawkins

Bournemouth Belle

*Basingstoke was a favourite haunt of the artist from 1964
until the end of steam on the Southern in 1967. It was an
ideal location to watch expresses roaring through and lesser
trains at rest. For good measure, there was also an interesting
engine shed to browse around. The Bournemouth Belle was
the last steam-hauled Pullman car train to run in Britain and
was the domain of the magnificent Bullied Pacifics until they
were superseded by class 47 diesels. Rebuilt West Country No
34042* Dorchester *thunders through with the Waterloo-
bound 'Belle' whilst an unrebuilt sister engine No 34002*
Salisbury *makes a smoky start with an up stopping train.*

Waterloo Departure

During their latter years the Southern Railway's Schools class 4–4–0s were regular performers on the summer Saturdays trains from Waterloo to Lymington Pier for the Isle of Wight ferry. One of these sturdy engines No 30903 Charterhouse *of Nine Elms shed stands in typical summer holiday weather at Waterloo station with one of these trains. The season is 1962. The last survivors of the class were withdrawn by the end of the year. The Lymington trains were their swansong. The Schools (or class V) were designed by R.E.L. Maunsel and introduced in 1930. They were, and remained, the most powerful 4–4–0 type ever built in Britain. The total of forty was built by 1935. All were named after well known public schools.*

8
STATIONS

TODAY you have to go to India to see railway stations used as a meeting place of all humanity. The time was that you could enter a station and immerse yourself in a spectacle greater than most modern tourist attractions for free, or were it a 'closed' station for an old penny.

Nothing has changed as radically as railway stations, large and small; but here the nostalgia is in the major termini and junctions of childhood memory or our parents' descriptions and experiences passed down orally. Memories indeed... of noise, glamour, dirt, excitement, theatrical activity between lulls, a hundred and one sources of interest and fascination (and temptation to spend your money).

It is perhaps recalling the sounds and noises of yesteryear's great stations that most emphasises the change. For a start even most male youngsters went through a stage (female ones were less able to predict what was going to happen) of being scared of locomotives whose safety valves might suddenly explode into a deafening roar or whose whistles might make you think it were the day of judgement. Boys of three or four could be seen trying to tug their fathers away from the front end of the train. Aunts who passed by engines — like everything else trying to ignore the surroundings — would, if caught by a sudden blowing of the safety valve or whistle, complain their hearing would never be the same again. Sometimes their forecast was right, for delicate human ears were not meant for such strains, often amplified under low station roofs. Tinnitus sufferers would certainly have a ringing in their ears for weeks to come. It was not just train engines that upset the peace, but all those shunters adding and detaching vehicles, an especial danger being the sudden coming to life of one whose crew had previously seemed intent on spending eternity in a bay platform or on a through track maybe at the end of a scissors crossover.

Gongs rung by signalmen to inform station staff of a forthcoming movement could also make you jump. So, of course, could the unhitching of the brake pipe when a locomotive was being cut off; generations of passengers arriving at Liverpool Street knew that the line's Westinghouse brake was particularly violent in its undoing.

Other sounds were friendly, and how we miss some of them... the wheel tapper instantly getting to work as soon as a train halted, paper boys and refreshment vendors 'shouting' their wares hoping to bring customers to the window, porters and postmen uttering the destination of parcels and bags being sorted onto lined-up carts and trolleys, some of the parcels (such as dogs, cats, day-old chicks, calves) themselves adding to the cacophony. The noisy movement of barrows often interrupted conversation and prevented you hearing what the porters were shouting. (Until the opening of centralised creameries which led to the conveyance of liquid milk in most areas just before World War II, manhandled milk churns let out excruciating noises… and some could still be seen or more usually heard well into the 1950s.) Often bells could be heard ringing in signal cabins; the messages of the platform gongs were ever compulsive if you were not too close to be frightened, and you listened for the sound of point movements, and signals being raised or lowered. Even point rodding and signal wires contributed their bit. Then everything would be drowned by the sound of a hundred chattering passengers rapidly pacing along the platform.

Different stations of course had their own smells. The kind of locomotive and the coal being burnt made the largest impact, but odours from breweries or other industries might contribute, along with livestock and perishables on the platform. Southern waiting rooms like trains had their disinfectant smell almost as distinctive as the acrid smoke of LNER engines. Gentlemen had their hair cut in underground salons beside lavatories whose pong could be detected well above ground. Refreshment rooms could attract with their freshness and newly-baked morning goods, or smell like stale pubs, and the air in waiting rooms ranged from that of a respectable hotel drawing room to that of the doss house.

As for things to see and do, they were endless. Consider how much has been removed from a typical station. For starters, a rich variety of train indications, from finger-pointing boards inserted individually into the brackets for each train of the day at many stations to permanent enamel displays of departures that would cover an entire timetable. Roller blinds might display only half an hour of departures at peak times but the entire quieter night

The arrival side at Paddington probably in the early to mid-1950s—note the pre-war cab on the left and Jowett car to the right. The locomotive is Castle class 4–6–0 No 7006 Lydford Castle *allocated to Gloucester Horton Road so presumably the train is from Cheltenham.*

period and list every calling place and connection of every train. Woe betide if the porter responsible for moving them on failed to do so. Elsewhere a board with each train's details was manually put on display, at Glasgow Central in a huge exhibition of train details keeping three or four men constantly on the trot at busy times. Posters listing departures and platforms at large stations had a supplementary 'Today's Arrangements' pinned on. Infrequent travellers tended to ignore the lot and ask—and then ask again to ensure consistency of reply.

Departures were only one thing the railways told you about themselves. Booking halls and enquiry offices were as fascinating as public libraries, and which of us has not collected a handful of pamphlets about new services and excursions for entertainment while on the journey or waiting for our train in the refreshment room. They did not have to be about journeys we were actually likely to make ourselves, since they always revealed details of a region's social and economic activity. Remember, too, that you bought the railways' own magazines and items like their annual holiday guides from the booking office. Then there were the posters. Around a large station you could see displayed the latest work of many of the best commercial artists of the day, posters now rare and expensive collectors' pieces. For good measure the Great Western displayed relief maps (Dartmoor no doubt formed out of deep papier mâché) while the ex-North Eastern lines on the LNER had ceramic maps of the former system, somewhat lavatorial but at least easy to clean. Both types survived well into the 1960s; a few still do.

The ticket collector chalked up whether trains were on time (often just T) or how many minutes late. Glass case models of the latest locomotives were waiting for your penny for charity, their driving wheels whirling for half a minute when so fed... and, joy of joys, at many stations you could not only hear the bells in the signalboxes (and telephone conversations if windows were open in summer) but actually see track layouts and levers being pulled. Remember when a major station such as the Midland's Leicester would have signalboxes within sight of each other, and when signals and scissors crossovers mid-way down platforms were common?

Waiting rooms were not the favourites of young enthusiasts but could still be rewarding in their furnishings, fires and posters (and also their complements of human beings). Even two-platform stations at resorts like Torquay had separate first and third class and ladies' rooms, while larger junctions segregated their classes if not the sexes even in the refreshment rooms, and it was not only *Punch* that suggested that sandwiches were fresher in first. You were, of course, never expected to have to cross by bridge or subway to buy a cup of tea any more than to relieve yourself. Each platform or island was like a self-contained borough within a city, a focal point being the bookstall.

Bookstalls often seemed a geometric confusion: papers, placards, magazines and books dangling, hanging, projecting themselves at every conceivable angle to supplement the main horizontal and vertical displays with never a vacant inch. Trade was prodigious, railwaymen and daily passengers creating a base of regular business with chance sales to occasional passengers on top. Frequently you could find items at station bookstalls not stocked in the cities or towns the stations served—such as newspapers published at

distant points served by the station (between the London termini you could find every regional daily) as well as publications about the railways themselves. Thousands purchased their first railway magazine (and usually *The Railway Magazine*, the only popular periodical devoted to railways before 1939) with hard-earned pocket money as part of a station expedition.

If you could resist the temptations of the refreshment room, and never even considered the full-fledged restaurant for a three-course meal that most sizeable stations also supported, you still had to pass the automatic chocolate machines. For many this was not so difficult since Nestlé's chocolate, which somehow had a monopoly, was not generally regarded as the best. A penny might be better spent on engraving your name or message on a strip of aluminium. Is memory accurate in recalling that you were allowed twenty-six characters or spaces? A penny was also needed to get to the toilet (apart from the gents urinals)... an expensive luxury. But then if the station were closed, strictly speaking your platform ticket only purchased the right to be present for an hour, though only occasionally would a mean ticket collector make a surcharge. Where surcharges were common, you might get

Liverpool Street is an 18 platform terminus just within the City of London and is divided into two almost equal halves. The Norfolkman is seen at platform No 9 on the west side, with Stratford-based Britannia class 7 Pacific No 70001 Lord Hurcomb *providing the motive power, in the early 1950s. The Great Eastern section used discs rather than lamps to indicate train classification. There were some local codes, one of which is seen on the L1 2–6–4 tank on the left.*

67

better value booking a journey to a neighbourhood station, one or two coppers enabling you to hop on to a train at most places when stations were packed tighter together. For the most part ticket collectors and porters welcomed your interest, and even the station inspector might guide you to the next point of interest as though he were a museum curator.

There were still many other things you could do: buy cards (and stamps from machines) and post them, platform letter boxes being cleared as frequently as any, telephone, buy an ice cream from a cart pushed up the platform... and of course help the old lady who had not immediately found a porter with her luggage, hoping to recoup the cost.

Porters were however usually in evidence. The biggest difference we would notice going back to a busy station of thirty or more years ago is not the trains themselves but the sheer pressure of people. Literally hundreds worked at larger junctions, not including those in the district offices through whose front doors staff were ever passing. Many big stations used to serve more routes than today; trains were often busier, waits longer—and it was much more common to be seen off or met by family or servants. You have to experience checking in at Heathrow on a bad day to remember what it was

Edinburgh Waverley platform 10 in the summer of 1961 with class A4 No 60024 Kingfisher *at the head of* The Elizabethan— *9.30am Waverley to King's Cross. Waverley is a large rambling station of 21 platforms with a relatively low overall roof no more than 42ft above rail level due to the legal restriction of 'Servitudes'—the Scottish equivalent of 'Ancient Lights'. The station is now partially electrified for both East Coast and West Coast services.*

like, and how much space luggage takes between waiting passengers. Remember when a smart porter would capture the luggage of half a dozen arriving or departing passengers, when mother would worry that the hat box balanced at the top of the pile would fall off and dad was ever counting, counting where everything was and then digging into his pocket for an appropriate tip?

Yet all this is like describing the stage set without the story or actors. While much life went on regardless of trains, there was never any doubt that it was really about arrivals and departures. Patterns were then quite different from today's. Preston, Taunton, York, Sheffield Midland, Perth... almost everywhere except in the South East, locals accounted for a high proportion of trains; expresses were infrequent and major affairs of great length (in number of carriages) and ceremony. The pattern was very familiar. After a siesta, a batch of local and branch trains would disgorge their passengers and parcels including produce of the countryside grown for city dwellers. While most passengers would surrender their tickets at the barrier, handfuls took advantage of the ingenious and often time-honoured connections to London or other distant cities. Often guard's vans were unloaded onto separate barrows for the main-line connection and local destinations and wheeled noisily away... having hardly got out of sight before a second two-coach train terminated at the same spot and other porters manoeuvred more barrows beside the opening van doors.

Everything came to life: booking hall, waiting and refreshment rooms, bookstalls, shunting engines. The engines took tail-end traffic (such as milk, gas tanks, and horse and cattle vehicles) off some of the local or branch trains and perhaps then attached themselves to a restaurant car to be added to the express. Steadily the main up platform, described by Arnold Bennett as the more modish, became crowded with passengers, railwaymen and luggage, the stationmaster in his silk hat emerging like an important second-line actor just after the gong had rung the requisite number of times and the home, starter and slotted distant arms of the semaphores had raised or lowered. Signals, like station furniture and the general state of well-being or decay, varied sharply according to railway and prosperity of the area.

Then the principal actor, the express: not just one of an hourly or bi-hourly pattern uniform with the others but an individual character with its own regular rolling stock and crew, and probably its antecedents deep in history if not running exactly to a time-honoured schedule. Whether or not officially named or nicknamed, each express had great personality, and its arrival—maybe fifteen coaches of it—justified the grandeur of the station. Ironically the frequency of services was much less at those great cathedrals of steam north of Birmingham than at the generally inferior stations (except London ones) in the South. Even most long-distance arrivals at Birmingham were real events (New Street and Snow Hill being as different as any two could be) while over at Leicester, an Anglo-Scottish express had onlookers as fascinated as the audience of any theatrical production.

Much had to be done in the few minutes expresses were halted. Passengers had to find their reserved seats, and even if not reserved would have to ensure they were in the right coach or portion of those trains going to various destinations. Men seeing their womenfolk off would try to select a compartment with 'appropriate' travelling companions. Those who wanted their own company looked for empty compartments at the front or back. Those disliking long walks through the corridor settled for a carriage near the restaurant car.

Major stops usually saw the restaurant car between meal sittings, and a red flag would go out to indicate that supplies were being taken on board. Such stops often brought a change of locomotive. A shunting engine might be attaching or detaching at the back, while porters and postmen struggled with barrow loads against the clock. A minute before departure it might seem that the train would never be ready but, encouraged by the inspector's whistle, miraculously a couple of dozen doors closed within a few seconds, the last to be held open perhaps being for a passenger who had shot off to the refreshment room for sustenance. We forget that buffet cars were rare even in the last great days of steam, the on-board choice being between a full meal (including perhaps a set coffee service) or nothing. If you did not take your seat in the restaurant car, you took your own refreshments or fled to a platform refreshment room, the knowledgeable jumping off from the nearest door. Those in charge of platform trolleys were also strategically placed to start business but often lacked time to serve the entire train.

Excitement was enhanced by several factors. Not only were there few expresses but many were the only service on its route or of its kind during the entire day. The next stop was often hours away; London itself having a vast range of places reached non-stop. To be on board you were really someone on a true adventure. Destination boards added to the glamour.

Longer non-stop runs meant occasional 'runners' rushing through. Exeter St David's, for example, had just as keen an atmosphere whether the Torbay Express was arriving non-stop from Paddington or the summer Cornish Riviera Limited was cleared for a full-speed run through the centre road. Throughout the land, when things went with the usual precision, tension rose as the last goods or local or shunting engine was tucked safely in the loop, bay or platform. The stop and distant signals cleared in quick succession, followed it seemed only moments later by the whistle of the express telling all to stand clear. At many locations, including Exeter St David's, level crossing gates had to be closed but pedestrians were allowed across only seconds ahead of the racing train. At Grantham, Doncaster, wherever, there would always be a huddle of onlookers to wonder in awe at the organisation that allowed the Flying Scotsman or the pre-war Silver Jubilee to pass uninterrupted on its exalted way... though of course a hot box on a preceding goods or even a parcel trolley falling off the platform did occasionally cause delay.

Precision timing: exhilaratingly, it happened day by day, week by week, much of the quieter time of the year. It has always mainly been passengers who delay trains, in steam days especially crowds often affecting locomotive performance by their extra weight as well as necessitating longer station stops. One reason why things more usually ran like clockwork is precisely that most of the nation's fastest trains had very limited stops. On some lines, but especially Great Western ones, the rule has always been the fewer the stops the better the punctuality, today's more frequent stops no doubt attracting extra traffic but inevitably affecting performance at busy times.

Birmingham Snow Hill was a much more salubrious station than New Street having been rebuilt c1914. Modified Hall class 4–6–0 No 6991 Acton Burnell Hall *is seen at platforms 7 and 8 with a relief portion of the Pines Express, reporting number 1O39, on 7 August 1965. The main train was diesel hauled by a class 47. No 6991 lasted to the end of Western Region steam working and was withdrawn in December 1965 from Oxford shed.*

and overcrowding of yesteryear yet often think fondly of their own or their parents' memories when getting there was half the fun. Indeed, even on the most congested summer Saturdays in the late 1940s and 1950s, people frequently spoke of the journey as being the best part of the holiday. They had never before seen such a kaleidoscope of scenery and human and farming activity as a long distance railway journey made available. Children who have not experienced all human life in a railway station have especially missed out. We even enjoyed many delays... especially those to local trains on peak summer Saturdays when everything might run two hours late including the departure of an all-stations-and-halts branch train from a bay not allowed out onto the main line until its appropriate slot between expresses. Less fun was being stuck in a non-corridor coach at a junction for an hour or more waiting for a spare platform. Now we see under-used if not abandoned platforms everywhere, but once it was platform rather than track capacity that was the limiting factor. Even on the generally well-regulated Great Western and its successor the Western Region, queuing to get into Paddington or Bristol Temple Meads might add twenty-five percent even to a long journey.

Strangely, in some areas a higher proportion of people occasionally use a station today than ever before. That is because more of us sometimes go to distant cities or their airports, notably London, and the train's specialist role is appreciated. But they mainly arrive in their own cars rather than on foot or by bus (or tram), and they lack yesteryear's mixture of excitement and apprehension. It would not occur to them that once the character of a town or city might be judged by its railway station.

LNER class D49/2 4–4–0 No 62751 The Albrighton stands in platform 8 at York station with a train from the Scarborough line, whilst a V2 class 2–6–2 waits at the signal on the down through road c1954. There is a carriage and wagon examiner checking the carriages adjacent to the V2. The layout of York station is now considerably altered following electrification and the removal of the through roads.

9

VILLAGE STOP

THE locomotive work had been exemplary. Though from the timetable it might have seemed a very secondary train, the streamlined West Country class Pacific had six well-used passenger and five parcels vehicles behind it. Departure from the junction was late, and driver and fireman were obviously intent on making up time. The uphill running was vigorous, the exhaust having a regular rhythm like the sound of a factory driven by water power.

Over the summit, and now the enginemen will surely have their reward. But as speed tops seventy a couple of miles on, the brakes are slammed on, and despite a long, plaintive whistle we are brought almost to a stand at the home signal and drift at walking speed through a deserted platform and beyond to the starter.

Silence. That is to say silence from the train, but gradually we take in the surroundings. On one side cattle are being driven along the lane for their evening milking, and close by on the other there is another lane leading to a field where a village fair is being held. We just catch the sound of the band, and decide to walk forward, our footsteps making almost everybody sitting in the compartments look toward the corridor before we are actually seen.

The guard has his van in the back of the front coach. 'Cattle on the line and the express delayed in front,' he tells us. We open the window of the very front door and are almost in the middle of the fair—or is it a village show. Almost at once the brass band comes to a stop, the musicians pack up their music, music stands and instruments and bundle themselves into a couple of shooting brakes, dashing off no doubt for an evening engagement.

Leisurely returning from the signalbox, the fireman informs his mate it is going to be some time yet. The driver alights with oil can, but perhaps more out of habit than necessity for no oiling is actually done. Maybe he just wants fresh air... but he quickly turns his attention to a couple of men standing near the fence. Escaping steam makes just sufficient hiss to prevent our catching the conversation. The refreshment tent has now been closed. Most people have drifted away. The village clock chimes six.

We walk back a couple of carriages and look out again. Making her way toward the lane, at the very end of the field immediately beneath the door, is a tall country girl in her late teens with bright cheeks, milky legs and arms and thick, dark hair which falls on either side of her head as she raises her hazel eyes and we say 'Good evening'.

Cautiously starting with pleasantries about the weather, the conversation turns to what kind of village this is and we discover she used to catch the train to school since the local one had been closed, though there are still two shops. One of the men who have been talking with the driver hears this and adds 'And three pubs'. Pausing momentarily on his way home, he lightheartedly warns: 'Now, don't be getting into trouble with fancy up-country folk, Betty'.

The smallest hint of a blush crosses her forehead and for a moment she seems to examine her shoes. Our own shoes being three feet above the level of her head, there is fat chance of 'getting into trouble'. Before we know if we are going to continue talking, the guard passes through the train. 'Sorry for the delay; we'll be away in a couple of minutes now.'

That frees our tongues. Names are formally exchanged. She likes riding horses and has her own pony. She got a prize at the village show... yes, it was the show with a bit of gymkhana in the field behind, but it was mainly over by tea time, though there is going to be a dance in the village hall.

'Are you going?'

'Nobody to go with. Nobody I want to, anyway.'

Now, there's a challenge. 'What time does it start?' Indeed, what time is there a train back, and how might we explain our non-appearance down the line. What might a taxi cost?

The reader will, of course, have guessed it. A rustling of a wire by the ballast tells that the signal has been pulled. Up she goes. We had not noticed the driver climbing back on board. In an instant she whistles and the wheels are turning, not even a fraction of a slip. Well, it is down hill.

'Nice talking,' she says.

'See you—soon!'—but it is too late to add more, whatever that might have been.

We will never know if she prepared herself for the dance, or turned up and was taken over by someone else, or whether she had children... or whether she ever thinks back to that lineside encounter.

Like girls in pigtails allegedly one-minded about ponies, we were supposed only to think of the diameter of driving wheels and cut-offs. Yet making the best of railways was a total experience and that meant at least acknowledging the existence of the opposite sex. What happened to the geography student going home to her colliery village from Swansea university to swot for finals? Or the girl on her way to Newquay who wanted to appreciate the moonlit Exe estuary from the corridor but spoilt things by revealing she worked for BR at Shrewsbury and hated their guts?

Most respectable young ladies of course did not look for compartments by themselves. Even restaurant car stewards seldom put both sexes together, though occasionally you might be in luck (if seriously out of pocket).

Once we had our regular girl friend, the joys of the non-corridor compartment of an uncrowded train were much to be savoured. Indeed, in the days when parents stayed at home, and home meant everyone in the same living room, where else could you enjoy upholstered privacy better than in the spacious compartment of a non-corridor train making only brief stops at deserted stations and halts? It was certainly better than going to the cinema... and that apart from the fact that, however passionate, you were still a railway lover. When worldly progression meant going by car, kissing stops were naturally lay-bys from which (without seeming to go off the boil) you could see the passage of the day's best express, perhaps double headed just having ascended a major incline.

Railways never were divorced from life.

76

10
LONDON MIDLAND

SHORTLY after one dirty tank engine shunts the last of the coal trucks clear of the platform, another unceremoniously arrives with a train of three non-corridor carriages. A few doors open, passengers alight and those waiting to join shuffle up and down the platform peering in to discover the least undesirable companions for the ride into town. Unable to see through the filthy windows, a couple of people open doors to establish what room there is inside. In first class a gentleman brushes the seat with his hands and places a newspaper on it before sitting, while next door two schoolboys swing their satchels onto the moquette and raise a miniature dust storm. The driver looks back waiting for the guard's signal; a curious passenger has noticed his engine is fifty years old and its paintwork so covered in grime that its number has been chalked up to make identification easier.

As the stopping train eases out, pouring sulphur into the air, this passenger looks around and notices that the station itself could do with a coat of paint rather than just a wash. Here is a place that nobody seems much to love; only the edge of the platform has ever been swept clean. Only a handful of the railway's own posters add a touch of brightness...

A typical London Midland Region express The Mancunian had a pedigree, if not a nomenclature, stretching back to the days of the old 'Premier Line'. A Camden-based rebuilt Scot No 46162 Queen's Westminster Rifleman *climbs out of Euston with the 6.00pm Euston–Manchester in the early 1950s. The stock is the very comfortable LMS period III coaches built from 1933 onwards, although the leading vehicle is of BR build, distinguished by the circular toilet window.*

An Anglo-Scottish express, the 11.15am Birmingham to Glasgow, ascends Beattock, without the aid of a banking engine, hauled by class 8P 4–6–2 No 46203 Princess Margaret Rose *in August 1952. All the coaches are painted in the first BR standard livery of crimson-and-cream. The locomotive is now preserved and based at the Midland Railway Centre at Butterley.*

inviting you to travel in luxury to far-away exotic places such as Llandudno, Buxton and the Clyde Coast. As a few more workers, school children and a couple of women with prams arrive for the next train, nobody daring to sit on the dust-laden seats, a whistle sounds and an express runs through the opposite platform. Hauled by a large, smart red Royal Scot class locomotive, it has eight or nine carriages including a well-filled restaurant car through whose windows you can see clearly. The destination boards displaying the train's route on the roof of the carriages momentarily evoke thoughts of distant relatives or reports of sporting events, but few of the passengers waiting to go into town have ever visited the places named or have any expectation of doing so during their lives.

The scene might have been at dozens of stations in England, Wales or Scotland immediately before World War II, or for that matter in the late 1940s. The LMS was a railway of contrasts: a veneer of respectability over an infrastructure of neglect; some of the world's best expresses and innumerable locals of unimaginable dirt; the best-kept main-line tracks in

the world and hundreds of stations whose neglect was beyond redemption.

The largest of the Big Four of the Grouping era, it was also the largest transport organisation in the entire world, the largest commercial organisation of any kind in the British Empire. Much of it was unbelievably humdrum, yet much of it had great glamour. When Henry Hall the band leader was wooed by the BBC, he took a salary drop of fifty percent from what the LMS was paying him as their principal band leader, normally based at Gleneagles. And if this seems surprising, it should be added that among the list of its 'biggests', the LMS ran the largest hotel chain in the Empire, regulating the top social life in many of Britain's most important cities as well as setting new standards of elegance from Stratford-upon-Avon to the Scottish Highlands. It also had a huge shipping fleet and was involved in every kind of industrial development.

'LMS: Hell of a mess,' schoolboys loyal to the other railways used to yell, yet it was the LMS traffic receipts that gave a quicker guide to the state of the nation's trade than any other single set of figures. In many ways it not only served great slices of Britain—from the mouth of the Thames and South Wales through the great industrial heartlands of the Midlands, North and Scottish Lowlands to the coastal extremities of Holyhead and Wick—but it *was* Britain. It had an importance hard to comprehend in

From 1958 to 1967 the West Coast main line between Manchester, Liverpool and Birmingham to Euston suffered much disruption due to the electrification and rebuilding of stations. This is Coventry station c1961 in a state of confusion with very few amenities for passengers. Two Stanier class 3P 2–6–2Ts are visible both apparently doing a 'House of Peers' (nothing in particular but doing it very well). Further along the down platform there is a two-car Metro-Cammell DMU.

today's motor and air age, and management problems that perhaps set the trend for loss of pride in the job that Britain has so dearly paid the price for in the competitive commercial world.

The railway was forged out of the compulsory merger of numerous companies of great individuality and different tradition. Though some of the others, such as the Lancashire & Yorkshire, were themselves very substantial affairs, in England the main pair were the London & North Western and the Midland, ever arch rivals. The LNWR advertised itself as the Premier Line and its main West Coast route out of Euston to the Midlands, North Wales, Manchester, Liverpool, Blackpool, the Lake District and Carlisle had a quality second to none. Autocratic, gentlemanly, placing equal importance on track, locomotives and carriages, it pioneered many world standards.

The Midland, out of St Pancras but governed from Derby, was a much tougher affair run by stiff businessmen, with some of the best carriages anywhere in the world but relying on small locomotives that whisked passengers in short, feather-weight trains... and of course earned its fortune carrying coal, by queues of daily trains to London.

There was no way the pair would work happily together, and it is interesting to recall that for a moment before Grouping the government toyed with having six rather than four companies, giving Scotland one to itself and making another out of the Midland and Great Central. But while it was felt right to force mergers and generally control the railways more effectively, since they wielded tremendous power, the ethos was that as well as being competitive they also had to be profitable, and it was feared that Scotland might not adequately support its own system.

As an example of the problems of forced marriage, the Midland men who immediately came out on top insisted that their view of locomotive policy was correct... insisted that since their own expresses were frequently double headed, those running out of Euston should be given a second engine. Stories went the rounds of North Western drivers being brought to tears when told they needed a second engine to do work that one had happily done before. Such arguments were coupled with changed promotion prospects for many and the loss of the much-loved individual liveries. While Midland red was adopted for express engines (and all carriages) lesser locomotives went black, and that alone killed much pride.

With a quarter of a million employees, over four hundred different classes of locomotive, three thousand goods stations scattered over a system of over 7,000 route miles in Ulster as well as England, Wales and Scotland, and major involvement in every region other than England's North East, the LMS was clearly going to be an administrative nightmare. Not even in the United States had anyone at that time faced such a management challenge.

It began badly, with internal squabbles, lack of guidelines and industrial troubles. Profitability started poorly and became steadily worse with strikes, depression, road competition and an inflexible government. Yet there were solid achievements, especially in paving the way for today's InterCity services.

In some ways the LMS never got it together, and arguably the decision to centralise management was the first and principal mistake. But it was at least partly rescued and energetically led by one of the most famous of all twentieth-century railmen, and also one of the least likely: Lord Stamp (as he later became), teetotaller, Nonconformist lay preacher,

This is a pure LMS train on the ex-Midland line out of Leeds in early BR days; the route was a London Midland Region penetrating line, which was later transferred to the North Eastern Region. BR-built class 5 4–6–0 No 44667 of Derby shed passes Holbeck Low Level with an ordinary passenger train for either Bradford or Morecambe formed of LMS corridor coaches.

writer of economics text books and company director via the ranks of the Inland Revenue. Astonishment at his appointment was increased by the fact that he was President (following the American example) though soon also became chairman and had the distinction of reporting to himself as he wielded huge, decisive power. Perhaps the prototype of eighties-style bosses, he paid himself well. When a shareholder questioned his £15,000, he retorted that it equalled a ham sandwich for each shareholder and 'I'm sure that you will not begrudge me my ham sandwich'.

Lingering power struggles subsided as Stamp made Euston the undisputed base: the old Euston of Gothic portico and lodge (through which our taxi used to enter) of cathedral-like Great Hall and separate arrival and departure stations. Standardisation was Stamp's watchword. There was little time for niceties; it was standardisation by blunt hammer, a sinister dress rehearsal for nationalisation, though undoubtedly Stamp would have been a better leader of BR than any that were available.

The particular achievement was on the locomotive side. In the early years there was a desperate shortage of power as well as extravagant variety of type. The turning point came when William Stanier (later Sir William) was poached from the GWR and produced successive classes combining economy with power, as well as giving the LMS a distinctive touch. By 1938 Stamp was able to boast that standardisation and increase in power had resulted in the number of

locomotives being cut from 10,396 to 7,688 and more importantly the number of classes from 404 to 162. A huge slice of the spending went on engines and their fuel (the LMS reckoned that its six and a half million tons of coal burned annually gave employment to 26,500 miners) and that performance was totally dependent on steaming at the 'front end'.

Even the Royal Scots of the late 1920s had been largely designed by an outside company, but Stanier made the LMS self-sufficient, the Empire's largest engineering capacity under single ownership at his command. New classes followed rapidly in the 1930s, and expresses were speeded up as they became heavier and gave greater comfort. The crowning success was the streamlined Coronation Scot linking Euston with Glasgow… in the days when only two daytime expresses offered passengers a ride at ordinary fares. While the LMS greatly increased inter-city travel it was from a low base, and throughout its existence people from the provinces were far more likely to visit London aboard a sporting or military special.

Facilities were also improved at locomotive depots. Anything grander simply could not be afforded as the railway struggled with declining receipts. Electric traction was confined to a few isolated routes, no

Johnson class 1P 0–4–4 tank No 58047 leaves Wells (Priory Road) for Glastonbury & Street with a pull-and-push service in 1951. The S&D branch closed in October of that year. The small Somerset city of Wells was for a short period in the 1870s served by three separate companies, each with its own terminus. The main S&D system closed in March 1966.

major stations were built or even modernised, and the accident record was poor. The hotels and catering side employing 8,000 people invoked even higher standards; passenger comfort was increased even on most local services (in terms of quality of ride and space between seats as opposed to cleanliness). The LMS is fondly remembered for grand trains and hotels and its art, but slowly most stations deteriorated until even those around London's suburbs were unbelievably shabby. And the basic geography remained unchanged. The LMS ran three of the four routes across the Pennines and had many penetrating lines. It was like an octopus, with penetrating lines to Southend-on-Sea and Carmarthen, to mention but two.

Had the trade revival in the last pre-war years continued, the LMS might conceivably have made good. But coal and staff shortages, enormous extra traffic demands and the death of Lord Stamp in a London air raid in 1941 meant that at nationalisation

Ashchurch on the Midland's Bristol line still displays plenty of pre-Grouping influence in this September 1952 view. In the goods yard a Johnson 0–4–4T No 58071 is shunting cattle wagons. On the main line an LMS-built, right-hand drive class 4F 0–6–0 No 44123 in early BR livery heads a freight train south. The second wagon is lettered 'Glyncorrwg wgns'. Note the bracket signals, one purely Midland the other an upper quadrant replacement.

the country inherited a poor train set covering many key areas.

The London Midland was perhaps the least loved of all the Regions. It began by basically taking over the English and Welsh part of the LMS but was subject to many boundary changes. Nationalisation made relatively little difference, for many LMS practices were initially adopted nation-wide but there was no strong identification or tradition to be lost. As Harrow & Wealdstone quickly showed, the system remained accident prone, and punctuality and

cleanliness were never remarkable. Though the LMR might take you to some of the most splendid scenery in North Wales, the Peak District and Lake District, some of its branch line trains were positively sordid. Many returning from Blackpool on excursion trains delayed by congestion at Preston or beyond cursed the fact that the Region delighted in making the most of its extensive stock of non-corridor trains. The Region seemed especially lacking in willpower to fight road competition in rural areas. Alone, it disallowed unstaffed halts, vigorously defending its policy that if traffic did not warrant the retention of staff then stations should close completely… as they sometimes did while being repainted or just accepting delivery of new seats or heating apparatus. Territory that had formerly been Midland seemed to avoid the worst of such depths, travel out of St Pancras definitely being superior to that from Euston. So late and overcrowded were many trains from Rugby that its folk generally abandoned the Euston route for Marylebone despite it offering much less choice of trains.

It was nonetheless the expresses that redeemed the Region. While few of us would have London Midland locals high up on our love list, the growing network of expresses was built on the firm LMS foundations of power, speed and comfort. The Premier Line (LNWR) had boasted the best track in the world north from Euston; that the London Midland certainly did not offer, had not maintained or rather restored after the war, but there was an attractive matter-of-factness in its generous and ever-increasing provision of fast trains. On many routes they seemed to come as frequently as suburban electrics at a time when you might spend 45 minutes beside the East Coast main line and see none.

It is thus not surprising that our London Midland images are mainly of powerful Pacifics hauling a dozen or more coaches. We of course especially remember them repainted in LMS maroon after the first BR red-and-cream livery in scenic settings such as the Lune Gorge before motorway days and Shap… and have a special place in our heart for the St Pancras to Scotland trains' passage of the Long Drag, the Settle & Carlisle. Sometimes, however, we revelled in the sheer ugliness of industrial areas through which the expresses swept like a breath of fresh air, and wondered how man could have contrived to produce such miserable settings as many of the Lancashire ones on former Lancashire & Yorkshire territory. But we also fondly remember the expresses arriving at and leaving the great junction stations, especially Crewe, with a sense of occasion and hubbub on the platform with which today's travellers are not familiar. Now you have to go to a busy market to get the same kind of feel. How they got those giant expresses of ten carriages carrying six or more hundred souls away with such little delay, and how promptly the station inspector's signal was responded to by guard and driver, had one in wondering awe.

The LMS introduced the concept of InterCity services and also those much hated words 'organise' and 'reorganise'. It was, of course, not far into nationalisation that the whole West Coast main line was thrown into turmoil with electrification and rebuilding especially at Euston and Birmingham New Street. We were perhaps more proud of rather than in love with the country's first long-distance electrics, but did undoubtedly enjoy the enhanced role the Midland route from St Pancras played during the transition, even though the much-promoted Midland Pullman to Manchester was an early diesel set, precursor of the 125s.

The crews of two class 3F 0–6–0 tanks Nos 47276 and 47502 enjoy a lively chat as they descend the Lickey immediately behind a freight train, under permissive block regulations, to save time whilst working Bromsgrove banking duty No 6.

Philip D. Hawkins

and how few trains are late; but even if we were ten minutes down the connections would comfortably reach their destinations on time. And as for those going to Perranporth, they have to cross over the bridge at Truro to get the local and change again at Chacewater with another 13 minutes wait there. It undoubtedly makes you feel special going to the far west. Yet we feel almost guilty dashing through Redruth and Camborne which served the industrial revolution so well and now form a single urban district with far more people than anywhere this train now serves. We sail through to Gwinear Road.

That might not be so ridiculous had not the three people changing there had to wait nearly half an hour for the branch train to Helston to get started... after the arrival of the stopper from Truro! We now see the white sands of Hayle and descend to St Erth where we change. An up train has just left, but it would seem to be too obvious to run a smart connection out of both it and the Cornish Riviera. We have to wait 13 minutes. Our mixed rake of corridor and non-corridor coaches hauled by another Prairie tank then shows off its superior role connecting with the day's best train from Paddington by being the only weekday service to miss Lelant Halt. Frustration about poor connections—the inevitable belief that we could organise it better—was always part of the enjoyment! But rounding the cliffs through Carbis Bay and on to St Ives any lingering negative feeling evaporates as the clouds, blue sea and white sands take our all.

Our only possible regret is that we have travelled on a weekday. On Saturdays the Cornish Riviera itself comes here. St Erth is then only second top (Truro the first) from Paddington, yet without change St Ives is reached half an hour later. No. We were right to miss the congestion but will photograph Saturday's arrival at what the stationmaster lovingly still calls Great Western on Sea.

The views across the bay open out to give a marvellous climax as journey's end at St Ives is reached. The 2.15pm from St Erth arrives at the terminus, 15 minutes later, behind GWR prairie tank No 4549 on Friday 4 August 1961. Another 4500 class 2–6–2 tank No 4570 stands in the bay platform. The small engine shed which closed at the end of the 1961 summer timetable can be seen beyond the last coach.

16
SUMMER

FOR thousands of railwaymen, railway enthusiasts, and those who simply used trains or depended on them for their business, the arrival of the summer timetable was a moment of excitement, even passion. Many staff could instantly tell what extra hours they might be working, and so what extra pay they would take home. Stationmasters jealously compared the services at their station with neighbouring and comparable ones. Everyone in the holiday business, but especially those responsible for publicity and attracting the visitors, could see what the railway was doing for their resort as opposed to rivals. Enthusiasts looked for accelerations, more Saturday trains (with restaurant cars working down more single-line branches) and oddities such as unbalanced workings or the repetition of a previous timing mistake. Regular travellers looked forward to faster, more comfortable journeys.

The traffic people had of course been conducting consultations since the levels of last summer's loadings had been noted, and timetable proofs had been circulated from top brass to stationmasters. But proofs were proofs and there could be all manner of changes. Even rumours of a new through Friday night train, or of a service experimentally introduced last summer not being repeated, could be awry. And while the public relations department put out their usual plugs, inevitably these selectively highlighted the gloss rather than the substance.

There was no moment in the railway calendar quite like the arrival of the finished timetable and having the joy or frustration of reviewing the detail that affected you. Most major service improvements, such as the further acceleration of key trains, began with the summer timetable which made it more glamorous than the winter one, quite apart from the fact that many more trains ran in summer. A growing number of branch as well as main lines were given separate summer Saturday tables, and scores of lines only saw Sunday trains in season.

Before the war timetables appeared as punctually as the crack trains they highlighted in their preliminary pages. During the war even the smallest stations received their copies on the dot, though the quantity printed was drastically reduced and you had to reserve yours well in advance. Though all railways but the Great Western now used reprints of the relevant pages from *Bradshaw*, each retained its individual preliminary pages with such items as summary tables (generously showing what the opposition also provided as between London and Birmingham or Wolverhampton). Until its last pre-nationalisation issue, 6 October 1947 (and until further notice) the Great Western retained its traditional 11½in by 7½in format and its own consistent but idiosyncratic system of notes (G for Saturdays excepted) for sixpence.

duties, while new carriages were hastily put into service and rakes of old ones that had hardly turned a wheel since last summer again readied. Before and after the war, the range of destination boards (some used less than a dozen occasions a year) grew steadily. Many railwaymen who reached retirement age earlier in the year were asked to stay on till September, while school leavers entering the railway profession were expected to start immediately. Just everything and everybody was needed for the coming rush.

The performance on the timetable's first day, always a Monday, was given special review… and on the six and nine o'clock news bulletins we expected to hear about the latest accelerations. VIPs were often carried on first runs. Space was usually plentiful, for the arrival of the augmented summer timetable did not automatically bring a huge increase in business compared with the previous weeks. The best journeys of all were in the early days of the summer timetable when everything was sparkling new but not taxed by peak season crowds. Without the need to run extras and split service trains into two or three, even the first Saturdays often went off smoothly. Do you recall in your entire life a holiday season whose business did not start unusually slowly?

At least until the end of the 1950s, the one thing never lacking in high summer was customers. What days they were, especially the summer Saturdays when record crowds were carried by day and night by a huge variety of routes and power was provided by a rich range of pre-Grouping, Grouping and BR Standard locomotives, freight as well as passenger. Though our elders might boast that in their childhood holiday trains were still more varied, especially in the liveries of their carriages, we had the advantage of far heavier traffic: more trains and heavier trains made possible

Blackpool expanded rapidly in the last century, with the visitors brought by the railways, to become the busiest holiday town in the country. Two large stations, Blackpool North and Blackpool Central, were required to handle the traffic from all over the country, but particularly workers from the Lancashire mill towns. This early 1930s view taken at Central is dominated by the famous tower opened in 1894 and shows a L&Y rebuilt Aspinall class 3F 0–6–0 No 12560, based at Blackpool Central shed (C32), shunting empty stock.

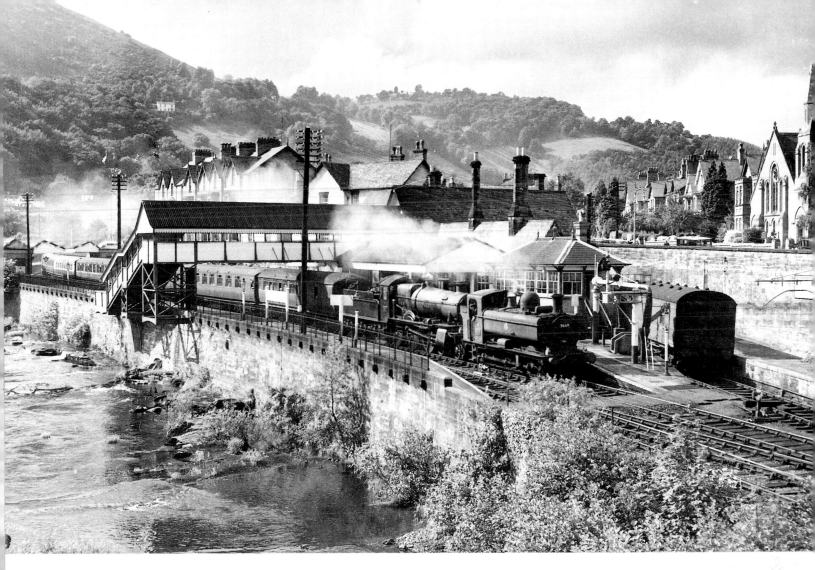

by the steady increase in power of the average locomotive. Of course there was never such a thing as the 'average', but these were indeed the days that drivers and firemen were frequently delighted to have a more powerful machine than in previous seasons. While today's speed is rationed mainly in terms of track and signalling capacity, with only occasional speed restrictions, most of the trains we loved went as fast as the steam locomotives could take them with reasonable economy in coal consumption. The cry was always for bigger engines. With 300 new steam locomotives coming out of BR's works annually (by 1954 three-quarters of them in BR's own classes) the power/weight ratio steadily improved. Yet double heading remained prevalent on many routes in summer, almost universal on some summer Saturdays... and our memory of the Lickey incline is perhaps of a 2P 4–4–0 piloting a Black Five and being banked by two LMS 0–6–0 tanks at snail's pace.

Mountains of Passengers' Luggage in Advance, the everlasting business of reserving seats or obtaining Regulation tickets where they were necessary, the standard Saturday restaurant car lunch of salad already laid on the table followed by cold dessert and coffee (whole trains of restaurant cars worked down to holiday areas on Fridays, each car to feed three or four sittings on a separate Saturday train back), most unusual pairings of locomotives, destination boards turned round to expose their blank side since not all stations

Holidaymakers returning from Butlins camp at Pwllheli enjoy the scenery of the Dee valley at Llangollen in the early 1950s. A class 5700 0–6–0 Pannier tank No 9669 pilots an unknown Manor class 4–6–0 on a train of ex-LNER carriages heading back across the country. Preservation, by the Llangollen Railway, has ensured this evocative GWR view is still intact today.

119

Lincolnshire atmosphere amidst spinning drivers and three-cylinder explosions. The A4s may have been sleek and fast, but they were also light on their feet. To be fair though, the ex-LMS Princess Coronations could have similar problems; on one occasion at Stafford, one of these superb Pacifics had great difficulty maintaining grip when starting a London-bound train, albeit of no less than seventeen bogies. Back on the East Coast main line, the other ex-LNER Pacifics seemed more sure-footed, and just as elegant in their individual ways. Added to these were B1s, B17s, V2s, 9Fs, WDs and a C12 (the Peterborough 4–4–2T station pilot) which appeared regularly there—a guaranteed feast of delights.

Back in those halcyon carefree days it was all too easy to become complacent. Steam ruled, had indeed done so since the beginning of railways, so the idea that change was inevitable, and indeed just around the corner, was not something that came to mind. Yet it should have been obvious, for on most days at Rugeley a foretaste of things to come was presented in sight and sound in the form of one of the prototype diesels, ex-LMS, ex-SR, or Deltic, doing the work of beloved steam locomotives which by then were having their last great fling. Perhaps it was all just a lingering dream.

B.R. 32735

BRITISH TRANSPORT COMMISSION
BRITISH RAILWAYS
LONDON MIDLAND REGION

YOUR REFERENCE

OUR REFERENCE

Telephone—

Telegrams—

....19......

Dear Sir,

VISITS TO MOTIVE POWER DEPOTS

With reference to your application for permission to visit Motive Power premises ; if you will kindly let me have the following information (giving at least 28 days' notice) by returning this form completed, I shall be pleased to give consideration to your application :—

1. No. of persons in party..........................
   (Permits cannot be granted to females)

2. Are you a male person over 21 years of age?............... If not, state your age...................
   (Persons under 16 years of age cannot be included in the permit unless in charge of an adult)

3. Give the ages of any members of the party under 16 years...

4. Is each member of the proposed party of British Nationality?...
   (Particulars of each individual to be given if an alien)

5. Depots it is desired to visit   6. Proposed date of visit   7. Proposed time of visit
   (In order of preference)

   ....

   ....

N.B.—Visits cannot be arranged on Saturdays, Mondays, or on the days immediately before or after Bank Holidays.

Yours faithfully,

....

....

....

Railway holidays very often commenced with the completion of this form. Hopes were always high that the application would be granted but very often requests to visit the busiest sheds would be declined.

18
NORTH EASTERN

VARIED indeed have been the celebrations, great and small, railway-oriented and about the comings and goings of the great and famous, at York station. But perhaps no informal gathering of the top management brass on the platform in the curved train shed had more poignancy than that on the first day of the 1948 summer timetable when the first postwar non-stop Flying Scotsman from King's Cross to Edinburgh passed through.

For a start the officials were proud of the fact that under the newly-established state ownership the North East had been granted its independence, the North Eastern Region, one of six, being the only English one to be governed from outside London. York was not just the obvious place for the Region's headquarters, but for any major railway institution outside London (the railway museum was indeed just down the road). At Grouping in 1923 there had been considerable disappointment that not only had the North Eastern Railway lost its independence but the new LNER had not thought it fit to set up its entire headquarters here. The announcement in 1947 that British Railways were to have a separate

Scarborough was the North Eastern Region's largest holiday destination and even in the 1960s handled numerous extra trains during the summer season. In this 1965 view, a York-based class B1 4–6–0 No 61319 pulls a train of empty stock into the station ready to embark returning holidaymakers. A DMU service, no doubt highlighted in the timetable, stands in the next platform.

clear barks and two fountains of smoke emerge as the train swings round the curve and has a clear run through the up platform. Another Prairie tank is piloting a Mogul, both giving their everything though still all-to-well below the speed limit of 40mph through the facing point with nine packed assorted carriages behind.

Though the sun has just dropped behind the hill, it remains warm and nearly all the windows are open, young heads poking through half a dozen or so. The little boy waves to each of the drivers in turn, and we see the train engine fireman show his driver the token before hanging it up on its hook. It must be a return excursion, perhaps 400 people returning to we do not know what city after a sunny day on the sands.

First the engines and then the coaches disappear into the cutting, but the exhausts blasting out the chimneys still echo around the valley as the signalman returns to his box with the token left on the automatic exchanger and 45 seconds later comes out with it to talk to the driver of the delayed down passenger. There is no sign of passengers on that; they might be out of view in corner seats, but certainly did not come out onto the platform. Experience tells there might be a dozen at most, and this cross is a reminder that country and seaside railways often carry more passengers on one special than a whole day's ordinary trains, Mondays to Fridays anyway.

Tonight is Friday, and the big day when nearly a score of trains, almost twice the Monday to Friday quota, pass through this station in each direction is tomorrow. Normally all passengers stop here, but not on summer

Manor at sunset over the river Wye near Brachney. On 17 October 1964, just a few days before its withdrawal, GWR Manor class 4–6–0 No 7815 Fritwell Manor returns to Gloucester with an evening freight from Hereford. The passenger service was also steam hauled, usually by a Collett goods 0–6–0, Prairie tank or Mogul and remained in the hands of GWR motive power to the last day, 31 October 1964.

Saturdays when the automatic token exchangers come into their own. But the only hint that tonight is Friday is the parcels van behind the standard two-coach branch line set: PLA, no doubt. For the uninitiated, PLA is Passengers' Luggage in Advance. It will be delivered to hotels and boarding houses and be waiting in the bedrooms of tomorrow's arriving guests much as passengers on cruises find their luggage in their cabins.

At last mother has persuaded the boy to walk home and we see them climb up the hill toward us. They have nearly reached us when the signalman again walks to the automatic exchanger, this time no doubt for the goods, the last train of the day, and normally the only one using the exchanger except on summer Saturdays. Mother and son greet us and nearly pass over the brow of the hill when we tell each other that 'Here she comes'. Mother realises that's that and pauses to talk while the lad asks if we saw the special with its two engines and is this the goods?

It is. Its 0–6–0 tender engine can be heard for miles around as it lifts about a score of trucks up from sea level through our station to the summit several miles ahead. Why the line is kept open for the goods, or rather why the goods cannot run earlier, within the time necessary to open the signalboxes to cope with the passenger traffic, is anybody's guess; maybe it is so profitable that a bit of extra expense does not matter, or maybe the junction's marshalling yard could not handle it earlier. One thing is for certain: it has run at this time for generations rather than decades, balanced by an early morning down goods. That also is meant to run non-stop, but the automatic exchangers are seldom used since the box ahead is not opened early enough to allow the signalman to clear the signals and get to the exchanger in time.

In the gathering dusk the signalman returns to his box for the last time, there no doubt to wait ten minutes for the train to pass out of the section and to close down for the night. Mother and son finish their conversation with us, female and male respectively, and we wave as we ourselves begin to pack. The railway dead, our attention is now freely given to the shimmering sea.

20
EATING EN ROUTE

Princess Royal class Pacific No 46210 Lady Patricia *climbs Shap with a heavy northbound express in spring 1949. A Stanier twelve-wheel first-class restaurant car (the LMS preferred 'dining car' prior to 1946) is placed fourth in the rake and the third-class open vehicle immediately in front of it will probably provide third-class dining facilities. Both engine and train are still in LMS colours.*

OF all the pleasures of railway travel, none beat having a meal in the restaurant car. Who did not feel the better, refreshed, more knowledgeable, better balanced, as the result of a good breakfast or just afternoon tea at speed?

Was it that we were always hungry? Or that we had little other experience of being treated with such respect? Or that we could see a wider spectrum of the countryside from the 'open' vehicle than in our own compartment? Or that we met interesting people? Or, indeed, that walking down the corridor on hearing 'Take your seats for second lunch' provided a refreshing change?

All of these came into it, yet somehow the total was more than the aggregate of the ingredients. You became immersed in the total enthralling experience, exhilarated that you ate good food with excellent service at speed through the ever-absorbing countryside, and yet took this exhilaration in your stride as though having a fish *and* meat course, and moving the glass away from the cutlery to stop the rattle, were the most normal things in the world. Part of the fun might indeed have been that you took for granted

much detail that many elders not used to eating at speed found distinctly novel. Many did not instantly comprehend the basic mechanics of the menu.

To which it has to be added that those able to take full meals were privileged. Excellent value though they might be, they were always expensive and beyond the means of many. You felt especially privileged sitting with glass in hand at the window when a train ran into a busy platform and those waiting opposite cursed their luck that they had positioned themselves where they could not get on.

Because of the expense of main meals, and especially the agony of having to do with a Plain Breakfast while others around you devoured their fry-ups, we often had to take our own sandwiches but treated ourselves to morning coffee or afternoon tea. They were not to be despised, for (apart from perhaps the issuing of a meal ticket) their serving involved all the elaborate procedure of the restaurant car: going there at the right time, perhaps just ahead of the official call, choosing an ideal facing window seat. You were served by a battery of waiters, asked politely if you wished more tea or coffee and then (as an individual bill was written) whether everything had been satisfactory. You were thanked for the tip—and stayed seated enjoying the ambience and the better view until it was obvious your presence was no longer welcome.

When funds allowed, what thrill it was to walk down the outside of the train at its starting station to request a meal ticket from the steward standing with packs in hand (one pack for each sitting) by the car door. Why was it always the 'car'? Down the train the steward would refer to the car as though every other vehicle was something different. The cars were often fascinating, frequently more venerable than the rest of the train. You might indeed be lucky enough to be served on a vehicle with six-wheeled bogies or be in the third class car separated by an entire kitchen car from the first class one of an LMS dining trio. Or take afternoon tea beside Loch Awe on the way to Oban in a former Pullman redolent of yesterday's luxury. Or enjoy a Gresley catering vehicle long after all others of his vintage had gone to the scrap heap. But you wanted to avoid being trapped in the windowless Bulleid tavern cars of the postwar Southern. Generally seating was more comfortable in restaurant cars than ordinary coaches, you were free from the nuisance of other people's luggage, and—as today—you were often seated first class when paying first-class fares was out of the question.

Part of the excitement was that generally you ate by the clock. On some Highland routes you had to take an early meal one way, and a late one the other, since the same car served down and up trains, its shunting from one to the other always adding interest. But even if you and the car made the entire journey, sittings were fixed according to traffic demands and staff convenience. Everlastingly there was pressure to serve you early, but where possible you waited for the last sitting, noticing when passengers from the previous one started drifting back to their seats.

Food was undoubtedly important, and usually (especially for those more likely to splurge on a meal on the move than one in an hotel) it spelt a reasonable degree of luxury. Immediately after the war menus were thin, the emphasis on chicken and tinned plums, but by the mid-1950s older passengers said the fare was as good as ever. Where else did you get such a breakfast plate, fish as well as meat at lunch and dinner, and so elaborate an afternoon tea? And what decisions! Fresh buttered toast or toasted tea cake? Dessert or savoury of a kind you would never find in any other eating place you patronised? After a pudding had been set down three times and the request for savoury repeated yet again, the parson opposite said that one would go through life a lot more easily conforming. Why?

Restaurant cars were not the place in which to be nobody. Better to be wicked, like dithering so longingly over the choice between buttered toast and tea cake that the steward gave you both, or to ask for cheese (always accompanied by celery the like of which again we never saw elsewhere) after pudding… or savoury after cheese. When the chief steward commented 'You like your savouries, sir' you felt really someone… and were relieved when you were not charged for the extra course. All of which perhaps does less than justice to the main courses. Meats and fishes were excellent, steak and kidney pies, for example, baked on the train with thick, crisp pastry and oodles of meat. Another touch of magic was that whereas at home and in most cafés and restaurants used in ordinary life vegetables were heaped on the plate, here you could decide which you wanted and which you could happily do without. While the peas were being chased round the bowl, you perhaps asked which was the train's balancing working, and so showed your interest in the railway and might later be told titbits of information, possibly about next summer's timetable.

Perhaps the best journeys of all were those on which one had successive meals at the same seat served by the same friendly crew. That was living. While conversation in the compartment was rare and when it happened often boring, only the more interesting people seemed to make it to the restaurant car and here exchanging views and information was ever welcome. To be told that one's company had been so enjoyed that could

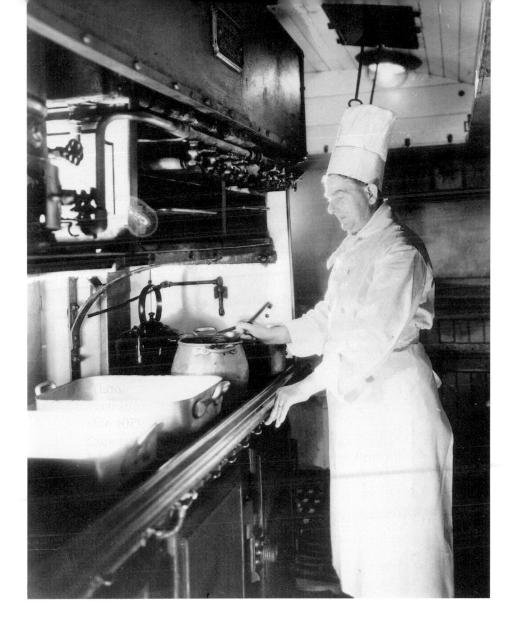

A chef prepares meals in the cramped surroundings of an LMS kitchen car. The summer 1952 LMR timetable advertised meals at the following prices: breakfast full 5s (25p), plain 2s 6d; both luncheon and diner were 6s and afternoon tea 2s.

one's bill be paid for was both flattering and made another restaurant car meal possible when funds were tight. Usually, of course, they were. Back home people who had never had the experience sympathised with us for having to make do with railway food, while we knew we were giving ourselves a special treat. (The fact that Dad treated himself but not the rest of the family to lunch on a 1930s Birkenhead–Kent express is still resented over half a century later. But one thing you rarely had to suffer in the car was the nuisance of other people's children.)

Over the years there was much fraternity with the stewards, as witnessed between them and guards, ticket collectors and those ladies who on the trains we loved went backward and forward making sure toilets were clean. Whether or not the restaurant were the only 'car', it was certainly the heart of the train... the place you visited for hot water or to warm baby's milk or even a bandage. The press made fun of the fact that a lonely American visiting Britain at the time of the Festival of Britain curtailed his exploring when he found friendship and comfort in the restaurant car to Hereford. He spent the rest of his vacation going to and fro, taking all his daily meals on board, merely filling in time during the London stopover. We understood.

21
SCOTTISH

FOR the Sassenach alighting north of the border for the first time, Glasgow is a wondrous place. The journey has been exhilarating, including lunch over Shap and afternoon tea climbing Beattock. The timetable has told us there are four termini, three with large railway hotels attached to them, and we know there is an independent underground nicknamed the Clockwork Orange, and that Glasgow is

An up freight hauled by domeless class 5 4–6–0 No 45168 crosses the bleak landscape near Dalwhinnie on the Highland line in 1955. The snow fences are to protect the line at this exposed location. The composition of the train gives an indication of the variety of traffic still being handled at this time.

the last stronghold of trams. But nothing prepares us for the pleasures in store.

It is still light when we roll across the Clyde into Central on a summer's evening a few years into nationalisation. There is no hurry to leave the station since we have a room in an outlying hotel booked and have been told what tram to take. We are amazed at the scale of activity on the sloping concourse. We have never seen anything like Central, with many of its platforms perpetually used by two trains at once and the massive display of details of departing trains, each train given a large placard put into its appropriate window by men who can be seen checking the

The last Pacific locomotive built by the LNER, class A2 No 60525 A. H. Peppercorn passes Ferryhill Junction as it leaves Aberdeen with the up West Coast Postal service for Euston on Saturday 16 June 1962. The passenger coaches at the rear form a Glasgow service. Eleven members of the class, which totalled fifteen in all, were based in the Scottish Region.

paperwork and making occasional telephone calls to ensure they get it right. At any one time there are a hundred people looking up at the display, while others continuously passing by glance up for confirmation they are going the right way. Each of the 13 platforms has its large, individual slot, so if there are two trains they are both included on the moveable placard with a clear 'Front' or 'Rear Train' before the list of stations served. To the left is space for special announcements and details of the expected punctuality or otherwise of long-distance arrivals, of which there are remarkably few. The whole display, occupying an entire floor above the restaurant, formerly general waiting room, is topped by 'Train Information' displayed in magnificent lettering. To the right of the restaurant, timetables are displayed and prove endlessly interesting.

Here is a truly major station but with only a handful of services for England. Most are going to places whose character we can only guess at... and many of which we have not even heard. The Cathcart Circle sounds so intriguing that we decide to put it high up on our priority list for the following days. But then the names of places to which there will be a steamer connection to from the Gourock express

sound as if they are straight out of a novel. We are amazed there even is a Gourock express, a full-length train with a 2–6–4T displaying express headlamps... and that soon there will be another, from the platforms furthest from that at which we arrived.

There is a wide roadway before these last two platforms serving the Gourock expresses and trains for Wemyss Bay and we walk down it, beyond the extensive glazed area and find a short platform which on an old plan is labelled the 'Fish, Fruit and Milk Platform'. From its end we can see everything coming and going. The sound of wheels hardly ceases, and when momentarily it does you can hear the points constantly being changed. Often three, four or even five trains can be seen moving at once if you look back into the glazed station, for it takes a minute for a short train nearest the buffers to emerge onto the bridge over the Clyde. Everything is steam,

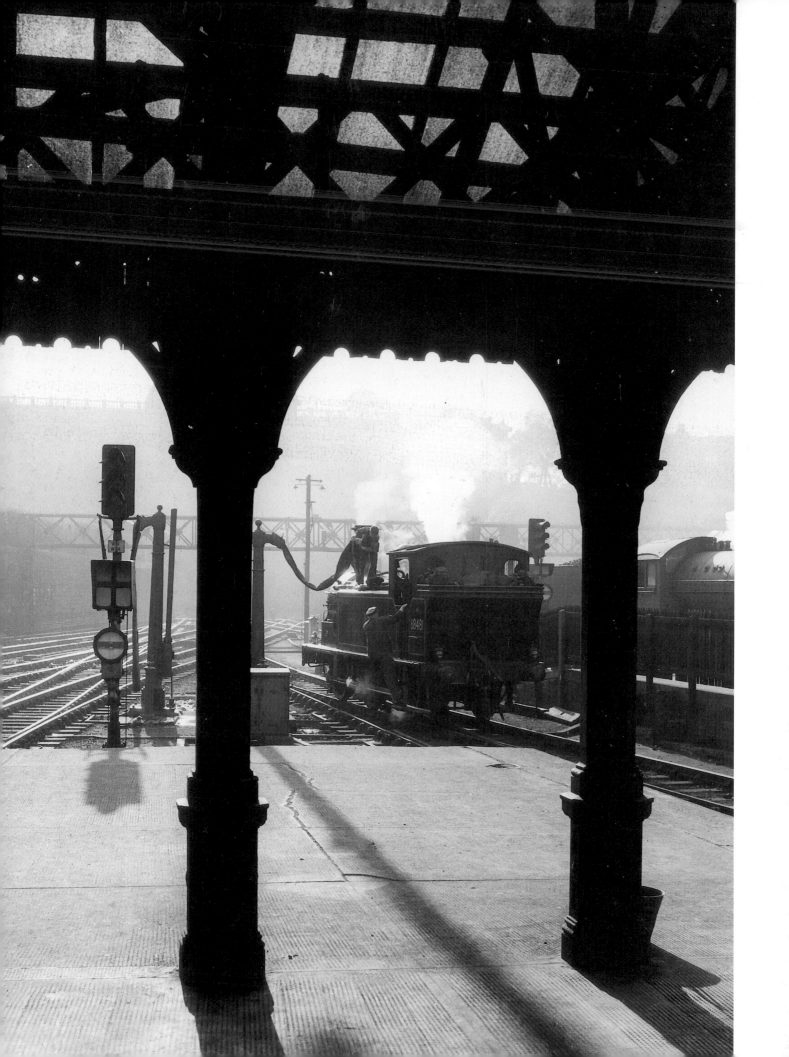

with some new BR Standard class tanks mixed with LMS and older machines some of whose like we have never seen before. Few would win marks for cleanliness. Much of the rolling stock is also pretty grotty, and trains on some routes seem very lightly loaded. Noting our interest in the last stages of the rush hour, the drivers of some of the light engines coming off one train, pausing shortly in a siding on the bridge, and backing onto a new arrival, wave their hands. These light engine movements are smartly made.

Walking back to the concourse, we note that the angle between the buffer stops of different pairs of tracks is at roughly 45 degrees to the station front. That and the slope, and the fact that every inch of the site surrounded by streets has been used to the full while giving an impression of spaciousness, make Central a real one-off.

An Edinburgh Waverley station pilot, class J83 0–6–0T No 68481, pauses for water in the early evening sunshine at the west end of the station. Six of these former Holmes, North British Railway tanks were painted lined black in recognition of their high profile duties at Waverley.

The world speed record holder for steam, class A4 4–6–2 No 60022 Mallard, *passes through Portobello c1958 with the prestigious East Coast non-stop service between London and Edinburgh* The Elizabethan. *The performance of the immaculately presented A4s on this service was keenly observed and recorded by both railwaymen and enthusiasts alike. The weight of the train, often over 400 tons, made this 6½ hour journey in many ways a much more exacting working than the pre-war* Coronation, *with formation weighing 312 tons tare.*

Overleaf above **Jersey Lily**

The Great Central main line out of Marylebone was the last major trunk route to be built in Britain and provided fast services from the capital to the east Midlands. J.G. Robinson's beautiful class 8B Atlantics worked the top expresses into the twenties and thirties and were considered by many to be the most elegant machines ever to ride the rails. Hence their popular nickname 'Jersey Lily', after the heart-throb actress of the time Lily Langtry. No 1086 in all her glory is seen here at Neasden engine sheds flanked by a pair of pom-pom 0–6–0s. When the GC was absorbed into the London & North Eastern Railway, much to the disgust of GC fans, many of these Atlantics were painted in plain black livery, and their shapely Robinson chimneys exchanged for a less flattering variety.

145

Above **North Western Style**

The London & North Western Railway made its locomotives earn their living and often hung loads on the drawbar that would have made other companies wince. It was also the first company to utilise water troughs and eventually had nine sets along the main line between Euston and Carlisle. Here, on Bushey troughs, a Precursor 4–4–0 No 1419 Tamerlane takes water while heading a heavy Euston to Manchester express in the early twenties. This engine was designed by George Whale and built at Crewe in March 1904, superheated in 1913 and eventually withdrawn from service by the London, Midland & Scottish Railway in March 1936. One hundred and thirty of these excellent machines were built up until August 1907. They typified the 'Premier Line's' locomotive design of the period.

Opposite below **North Eastern Elegance**

The North Eastern Railway was, in many ways, the most substantial constituent of the LNER. The locomotive designs by Sir Vincent Raven provided substantial motive power. His handsome Z-class Atlantics were introduced from 1911 and operated express services over the North Eastern section of the East Coast main line until superseded by the Gresley Pacifics from the late twenties. No 2201 is seen making a thunderous departure from Darlington just prior to the grouping of 1923.

Pacific Parade

The country end of platform 10 at King's Cross was a mecca for train watchers from nine to ninety, generation after generation gathering to witness spectacles such as this. The period is the mid-fifties as a Gresley A4 takes off with the Tees–Tyne Pullman whilst a Peppercorn A1 No 60131 Osprey *waits to follow on with an express for Leeds and Bradford. Locomotives had to work particularly hard out of King's Cross up the steep gradient through Gasworks and Copenhagen tunnels. The cacophony was music to the ears of platform-enders. The A4 depicted here No 60015* Quicksilver *did not survive the cutter's torch but happily five sister engines did. All of the A1s were scrapped but at the time of writing there are plans afoot to construct a brand new engine from the original blueprints. What an achievement that would be.*

TEES—TYNE
PULLMAN

60015

A-4

Philip D. Hawkins

were we to see such luxury on British rails secured simply by paying for a ticket, albeit including a supplement.

However, express trains generally improved dramatically during the Grouping years, in a way that by and large locals did not. And at nationalisation, when Scotland was given its own Region, it was obvious that those foundations would be built upon as soon as better times returned.

Scottish joy at having its independence was considerable, but while the North Eastern Region was poised to take instant advantage of York's regained freedom, north of the border there was an inevitably painful merger between the former LMS and LNER interests. Schisms went deep... from top managerial level to the men on the ground. Hardly anyone was satisfied. Though the first chief regional officer was an LNER man living in Edinburgh's North British Hotel who hardly set an example—not merely by refusing to move to the new Glasgow headquarters but doing the daily journey from railhead to railhead in a chauffeured car; at first it looked as though LMS interests might win. But one by one other former LNER men took key posts, and ultimately the LMS inheritance was considerably less treasured than the LNER one, though both suffered enormously.

This is not the place to recount the story of the especially severe Beeching cuts in Scotland and the closure of the LMS road to Aberdeen. The trains we loved mercifully ran ahead of that period of disaster, from which it has to be said the Scottish Region did eventually emerge with its own unified style and commercial drive... but that is even further in the future so far as we are concerned. We did enjoy the short-lived initial success of the Glasgow blue electrics, most starting on 5 November 1960. Traffic shot up in a gala atmosphere reminiscent of line openings of Victorian days, but next month we heard with horror that they had had to be withdrawn for technical reasons and all the old steam locomotives and their rolling stock brought back—for what turned out to be a painful ten months.

The Scotland we loved, while nearly everything was still steam, saw steadily accelerating expresses, freight as well as passenger. Innovations included the popular cheap-price Starlight Expresses from Marylebone to Edinburgh (Waverley) and St Pancras to Glasgow St Enoch (eventually as many as half a dozen packed trains a night), car-carrying sleepers and observation cars on the great scenic routes. The number of day and night trains from London by East and West Coast routes was far greater than before the war, while internally the Glasgow–Aberdeen service (including three top named restaurant car trains) combined comfort, style, speed and reliability... ultimately with Gresley's A4 Pacifics when they were replaced by the Deltics on top-line duties on the East Coast from London.

All this, and hardly anything had been lost. The excursion programme, especially from Glasgow, was as generous as ever, with numerous combined train/bus/ship services. The Waverley remained the pride of the North British's 'other' main line, from Carlisle to Edinburgh, while the famous Thames–Clyde Express also from St Pancras still served the G&SWR route from Carlisle to Glasgow. Though actually in England, Carlisle was one of the most colourful of 'Scottish' stations, with two main lines from the south and three to the north, plus the Port Road to Stranraer (an early casualty but then still carrying the nightly sleeper for Northern Irish passengers) and the cross-country line to Newcastle and the ex-LNER branch to Silloth.

Glasgow and its environs could warrant a fortnight's holiday if you let it. Edinburgh Waverley was one of the most marvellous of places, and if you ever needed a change you could sit in Princes Gardens watching the everlasting stream of expresses, locals and freights pass out of the tunnel and along the quadrupled track into the station. Perth was another joy, a real crossroads with endearing touches such as its own range of expresses to and from Euston, early car-carrying trains, heavy Post Office business and a frontier atmosphere, for everything going north of here seemed to linger to gain strength before setting off. It was not as varied especially in carriage livery as in earlier time, but in the course of a few hours you seemed to cop the very oldest and the very newest that BR had to offer. That included short pick-up goods that clearly were not going to survive much longer and some of the new vacuum-braked freights which gave a greater impression of permanence than later experience justified.

Of the lesser junctions, Crianlarich always springs to mind. In fact it was hardly a junction, for only after the introduction of diesel multiple units did one offer a day trip from Glasgow to Oban coming down the West Highland and switching to the former Caley

road here. The ex-Caley one-platform Crianlarich (Lower) was deemed one of the least important calls on the old Callander & Oban, romantic a route though it was in total. But the West Highland's island platform reached by underground passage and including (as it still does) a tea room attracted anyone with the slightest railway interest passing through by car, while if you were a train traveller you dashed off to make the best of the ten-minute refreshment stop in the days that the restaurant car only served full meals.

And the branch lines! Not merely were all the great scenic routes open, but many sprouted enthralling branches. Changing from the Oban train to either Killin (its locomotive shed in a dead end a mile beyond the station at Loch Tay), where shunting was normally by gravity, or Ballachulish perhaps was only

West Highland-based K2 2–6–0 No 61788 Loch Rannoch *eases out of Fort William yard during shunting operations c1952. Its home shed (63D) can be seen in the background. All the K2s transferred to Scotland received side window cabs and in addition 13 locomotives were named after lochs close to the West Highland line.*

a touch less exotic than taking the Light Railway from the Mound to Dornoch. You needed to immerse yourself in the timetable to make the best of scant connections, and even to understand the basic geography of the GNoS's connections at Cairnie Junction (like Killin Junction only an exchange platform without road access). In the reverse direction, you could say farewell to a friend as the train was divided into two parts at Elgin, and get together as it was joined up again 70 minutes later. The Coast line gave gorgeous views of fishing ports and resorts, but

St Margarets Sunset

Edward Thompson's B1 4–6–0s were intended as the LNER's 'go anywhere', 'do anything' mixed traffic locomotives and eventually totalled 410 engines built between 1942 and 1950. They replaced several life-expired 4–6–0s and 4–4–0s from all of the constituent LNER companies. One of the named members of the class, No 61244 Strang Steel, *is seen in the golden glow of the evening sun in the shed yard at St Margarets depot, Edinburgh, in the early sixties. This painting was created from notes and photographs taken on several visits to the depot in steam days. 61244 was a St Margarets inmate. For many years the artist pondered the meaning of this odd name until he discovered that Mr Steel had been a director of the LNER.*

the restaurant car went by equally attractive distillery country. Taking the train across Buchan brought the joy of passing one or more fish trains heading for England (unless there had been a storm) and fitting in the brief ride on from Fraserburgh (with its neat terminus with wooden booking hall) along the sands to St Combs. Every train to St Combs had its locomotive fitted with a cowcatcher. While you could see a much smaller percentage of Scotland's than England's coast from the train, there were other great stretches, on the main line to Aberdeen built on the cliffs with bridges over frequent gullies, and at several points on the North line but especially at Brora.

Fixing itineraries took so much time that we tried to do it before leaving England. We enjoyed the timetable footnote saying a train would stop to uplift passengers if timeous notice were given, but found we had not properly understood another footnote, or find that there was a cheap offer locally for a circuit we had thought would be too expensive. The type of trains and scenery, time, money, food, overnight accommodation all had to be taken into account. When we could afford it, we delighted in the first class freedom of Scotland ticket, whatever it was then called. Even cheap day tickets had their first-class version… though good use could be made of the new single second-class sleeper cabin from King's Cross to Edinburgh which alas did not last long.

We were always treated with great civility by staff and other local people… and not infrequently invited into signalboxes or onto footplates. It was sad to see traffic on lesser routes drop away sharply after the first few seasons of nationalisation, though even when the public had largely deserted the former GNoS branches it was still enjoyable enough meeting other enthusiasts who seemed to provide most of the traffic.

The greatest thrill was arriving on an overnight train from the South at Edinburgh, Glasgow, Perth, Aberdeen, Stirling or Inverness (we never made it on the once-weekly sleeper to Oban, and the West Highland was altogether too special to sleep on) and seeing the different landscape, the single-storey cottages and crofts, and sniffing the sharper air. You can still do it… indeed still alight on the platform and pick wild raspberries and roses while waiting to cross a train in the opposite direction—and who should discourage today's travellers from making the most of what is left? Yet in our hearts we know we were privileged to enjoy the very best days when steam was just one of the links deep back into history, when every station had its smiling staff waiting to please, and we were taking the most adventurous journeys any of our family or friends had yet even contemplated.

There was, of course, a down side. Some things, like restaurant car meals, tended not to be so good north of the border. Once Springburn had supplied not only much of Scotland but the world with its locomotives from the four great works crowded into a square mile of Glasgow suburb. Decline there was early, and sadly Cowlairs works came to have a poor reputation for the quality of its maintenance work, though this (and the contrast in quality provided between it and the ex-LNER works) became more evident in diesel days. Perfection you seldom had. Few of us complained about the overall picture in the 1950s.

This map is reproduced from the reverse of a Holiday Runabout ticket for Area No 18. Issued at Elgin on 1 July 1957 it was valid for one week and cost £1 third class. In fact third class had officially become second the year before.

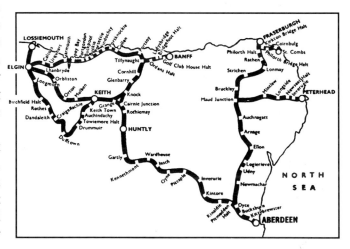

22
AUTUMN

IF there is a steady time of year on the railway, it is the autumn. First the state and then private schools are back, the winter timetable is in operation, freight business is buoyant and at least for the next couple of months there is little chance of a major weather-related catastrophe. If punctuality is not good now, it never will be.

As the steam-heating season begins, many passenger trains shed a coach: it is commonly stated that heating uses as much steam as carrying the extra load. There is little overcrowding and at most junctions trains are arriving embarrassingly early; if only this quality of journey could have been offered at the end of July and beginning of August. Restaurant car crews however look forward to brisk business. This is their busiest or at least most rewarding time of year as the captains of industry do much of their annual business travel and well-to-do provincials go to London for a show and to shop. The Motor Show and other exhibitions stimulate business, culminating in the Fat Stock Show at Smithfield. From much of Britain that provides restaurant cars with their largest wine bills accompanied by the year's most generous tips.

Workers' trains are running like clockwork (embankments even of electrified lines are mowed by hand so there are few trees shedding problem leaves), and early closing days see many towns sending large contingents to the nearest city for entertainment and shopping. It is all just as it should be: cosy, efficient, lacking in high drama but still varied. Saturday-only last down trains on branch lines become the busiest of the week. But in some cases that is because there is not a comparable bus. The writing is alas on the wall for many branch lines. Indeed, from even before nationalisation the last day of the summer service has seen the last trains on more lines, but it is still only those that can never have paid their way that are yet threatened.

Let us say it is 1954, and on the freight side optimism is almost total. 'On British Railways, improved recruitment of traffic staff, better wagon availability and turnaround, and adequate engine supply should go far, with improvements such as a more extensive use of alternative routes for goods trains and reorganisation of marshalling yards, to ensure smooth freight working.' The yard master invites a reporter from the local paper to see for himself. Freight trains are running longer distances without stops and serving more destinations without remarshalling. Typically a city of 250,000 people despatches a freight every 45 minutes from mid-evening until breakfast time, with about half that level of activity during the day. Though groceries are increasingly being delivered by their manufacturers' C-license lorries, overall business is still increasing to record levels. The forecast total traffic is 180,000,000 tons, nearly 2,500,000 more than last year.

Overleaf above
Fighting Duchess
Beattock Bank in Dumfriesshire has been immortalised over the years by the work of many fine photographers gracing the railway press. Among the best was the late Bill Anderson whose wonderfully lit shots taken at this location certainly made an impression on the artist. The year is 1938 and Princess Coronation Pacific No 6232 Duchess of Montrose *is virtually brand new. She is seen tackling the gradient near Greskine with a fifteen coach express helped in the rear by a 2–6–4 tank from Beattock. The crisp and even snow is interrupted only by the orderly footprints of a lineman who has disappeared into the distance. By many observers Stanier's Duchesses in this form were considered to be the pinnacle of British steam locomotive design both in appearance and performance. They were certainly handsome machines.*

157

Philip D. Hawkins

Opposite below **Scotch Goods**
Freight traffic, or goods as it was then known, was the life-blood of most railway companies. This was especially so for the London & North Eastern Railway. The express service from London to Scotland, the 'Scotch Goods' as it was popularly known, was a fine example of commercial acumen being served by dedicated staff. Worked by top-link engines, including Pacifics in later years, the goods was timed to express schedules. The Gresley V2 No 4774 is almost brand new as she sets out from King's Cross yard with the express goods in 1937. The Great Northern, like many railways of the day, was well blessed with attractive lattice-post signals and the imposing example here provides balance to the composition.

Above **Waiting in the Night**
There is something intoxicating about railways at night—especially with steam locomotives. The artist has vivid memories of lying in bed as a child and watching the orange firebox glow, and leaping sparks dancing to and fro past his bedroom window, the crew silhouetted against the glare with the fireman hard at work with his shovel. Surely many 'old masters' would have had a field day with such an evocative subject. Here, at Washwood Heath yards, Birmingham, a Stanier 8F No 48197 waits for the road not long before the end of steam in this area.

159

Ancient and Modern. Dean Goods 0–6–0 No 2411 turns south off the Great Western main line at Thingley Junction with a Swindon to Westbury freight in 1952. In the background the second Western Region gas turbine locomotive, built by Metropolitan Vickers, No 18100 heads the up Merchant Venturer for Paddington.

Carrying that calls for dedication and much unsociable work. Drivers and firemen of freights as well as passenger expresses are still subject to double-home working, and though more trains are partially 'fitted' (with vacuum brakes) guards have to alight from their vans at Stop Boards to pin conventional brakes down, the locomotive then pulling the trains down hill against the force of the brakes which have to be picked up at the foot of inclines. Some people say British Rail should have gone in for Continental-style bogie goods vehicles, but the rigid-based 4-wheeler is preferred for its cheapness and flexibility. Well over 50,000 of them are being built this year. Each hundred or so yards of street effectively owns several coal trucks.

Coal stocks are being built up for the winter, and the railway has won some business that used to go by coastal steamer, which proved unreliable in the 1947–8 winter. The yard master quotes other facts. Steel, that necessity of modern Britain, is on the up and needs another 3,000 trucks this year. Locomotives are more powerful, morale good because wages are higher and some weekend work has been curtailed. This yard which in LMS days used to work continuously is now twice the size but closes at lunch on Saturday till the early hours of Monday morning. That helps recruitment. Before the war everyone wanted to be a railwayman but now it is more difficult.

Traffic buoyancy is reflected down the branch line. Coal is the universal staple but each route has its specialities. Cement and quarry stone are on the up over much of upland Britain, sugar beet in East Anglia, teasels in Somerset, fruit from Kent and the West Country (who can forget the smell of the Tamar Valley strawberry specials?). Early Saturday morning hop pickers' specials from London to Kent are still great social events, and the hops they pick along with those from Herefordshire pour into Burton-on-

An up express freight, with loaded cattle wagons marshalled behind the locomotive, passes Charfield on the Midland main line from Bristol in the early 1950s. Motive power is provided by class 5 2–6–0 No 42872 of Derby shed (17A); its tender still carries LMS markings.

Trent, to be carried again as spent hops. Snape Maltings at Aldeburgh are not yet devoted to music but served by several trains a day at this time of year. Barley is being delivered to the Highland distilleries. Milk having to travel more than a hundred miles almost universally goes by train, as do horses. Lambourn and Newmarket head the places where a supply of horse-boxes is always on hand; in the mid-1950s up to a thousand new horseboxes are being built annually, the Western Region sticking to its own design. Scores of cattle trains run from ports served by the Irish ferries and from the English shires. In Ireland itself probably more head of cattle and horses are on the move than human beings, certainly outside the big cities.

We stop for lunch at a pub by a country station in Herefordshire. While our parents see what is on the menu, we watch the arrival of the down freight, with fifteen trucks between Dean goods and GWR guard's van, the station truck in the middle which squeaks to a halt outside the parcels office. There is a kitchen mangle along with pieces of farm apparatus, canisters of liquid gas, and crates and boxes that reveal little except the desire to improve living standards. The railway is benefiting from the increase in mail order catalogue buying. 'Better be off on your way,' says the signalman when assured the engine does not need a drink, 'and drop what you have for us on your return. There's a couple of hops to make the real stuff for you to pick up then. The special's right behind.'

Parents come out of the pub to say it is too busy with cattle dealers but, on seeing that display of disappointment that only a boy about to be deprived of seeing his train can make, decide there is no hurry after all and they might as well enjoy the 'local colour'. Indeed, as the special with eighteen cattle wagons arrives behind a Prairie tank, a sandwich is delivered and commented on by cattle dealers coming to the station to do the paperwork of conveying their purchases to Birmingham or by farmers just come to use the lavatory. 'Better eat that up here,' says the signalman.

The footplate crew of the special also come to the box, for social exchange of no practical purpose, but give an invitation to join them running round the train. Three blasts on the whistle as we clear the points at the up end of the loop has several farmers jump at the cattle pens below the embankment where the auctioneer is intoning away. Before parents finally run out of patience passengers and parcels start arriving for the up passenger that will be the first of three trains following each other to civilisation. Parcels include several trays of mushrooms and a crate of rabbits, legs up. 'Used to be lots more before myxomatosis.'

In a strange city that night sleep is impeded by the constant banging of trucks in the marshalling yard and occasional whistling of locomotives. On a crisp, windless night, trains can probably be heard by two-thirds of Britain's population, though perhaps only four or five million as noisily as this. As autumn proceeds (half term giving a sharp one week boost to passenger business) another railway noise wakes people up: the fog signal. Autumn may begin smoothly, but seldom turns into winter without fog. If the wheels are slowed down, much of the blame no doubt rests with the railways themselves as thousands of locomotives pour soot into the atmosphere... often a score of them under Liverpool Street's roof alone and many more at other London termini and locomotive depots. You notice it even in Devon: the

morning sun brings golden hues to a village, but five miles away Newton Abbot with its locomotive depot and coal-fired electricity works has a miniature smog making it silly to wear a white shirt.

But even around London and in the industrial Midlands and North, fog is generally only a railway irritant rather than a crisis. Newspapers and mail are delivered on time and few office workers arrive late. Though only the Western has its Automatic Train Control, rear-end collisions in bad visibility are rare, that at Harrow & Wealdstone in 1952 being exceptional in its consequences—a double collision killing well over 100 people, and giving impetus for an improved nationwide ATC.

Autumn ends on 21 December with the Christmas rush. Though it is not usually said of autumn, it comes in like a lamb and goes out like a lion, traffic being busiest when days are shortest and the weather most fickle.

The Southwell 'Paddy' pull-and-push service awaits the right away on its last 2½-mile journey to Rolleston Junction with the 8.30pm train on Saturday 13 June 1959. From Monday 15 June the service was withdrawn. Last days' of service and line closures were soon to become a common feature of every change of timetable, with many occurring with the introduction of the winter service in September.

23

TO BEYOND
MIDDLETON TOP

IT was that doyen of branch line photography, Arthur 'Cam' Camwell, who clinched the matter. 'North London tanks? Of course they are still at it!' What he meant was that these veterans, even in the early 1950s, were still double heading just half-a-dozen goods wagons up the steepest incline in the country, the 1 in 14 at Hopton between Middleton Top and Parsley Hay—two magnificent Derbyshire names to get your tongue round—every working day. And, to make matters even more interesting the very last LNWR 'Chopper' 2–4–0 tank was 'at it' too, working the short level section between Sheep Pasture Top and Middleton Bottom. Rather like an animal at a safari park, No 6428 was trapped on the section. It could only escape by being lowered down or hauled up a rope-worked incline.

In the mid-twentieth century the Cromford & High Peak line was certainly an anachronism. But then it was so even ninety or so years earlier, when it was acquired by the London & North Western Railway. The original intention was to link the Cromford and Peak Forest Canals by the High Peak Junction Canal from Cromford to Chapel Milton. The route via Grindleford, Hope and Edale, which included a tunnel 2¾ miles long, was surveyed by John Rennie in 1810, but failed due to great expense.

A more practicable alternative (but only just!) was a railway. The Cromford & High Peak Railway was incorporated by Act of Parliament on

The Cromford & High Peak line was a quaint survival into the 1960s having two rope-worked inclines and the steepest adhesion bank in the country—Hopton, 1 in 20 steepening to 1 in 14. In the early 1930s some ex-North London Railway 0–6–0Ts were drafted in to replace ageing LNWR 2–4–0Ts. LMS No 27527 was the Cromford Wharf shunter and is seen at the foot of Sheep Pasture Incline c1947. Visible through the A6 road bridge is the catch pit built to derail runaway wagons.

2 May 1825. The line was opened in two sections, from Cromford Canal to Hurdlow (foot of incline) on 29 May 1830 and on to Whaley Bridge on 6 July 1831.

There were nine inclines worked by endless chains powered by stationary beam engines built by The Butterley Company. Originally the sections between the inclines were worked by horses but locomotives were introduced in stages from 1833. A passenger service of sorts ran from 1833 until April 1876. It is not clear whether this was a horse drawn coach or locomotive worked, and the mind boggles at the thought of passenger coaches being worked up or down 1 in 8 gradients with a single chain the only saving link between life and death. The real traffic, however, was stone from the quarries along the route.

The C&HP was leased to the London & North Western Railway for 999 years in 1861, complete amalgamation coming in 1887. The Premier line had no other such oddity, but as narrow-gauge systems and other oddities, even the Liverpool overhead, closed it seemed an ever-stranger survival and attracted ever-more railway lovers. Some of the latter even travelled—standing up—by special train in London Midland Region days.

If one started at Cromford and climbed north westwards, the first leg meant using the inclined plane to Sheep Pasture at 1 in 9 then 1 in 8. By big railway times this formidable climb had become double track with steel cables replacing the old chain. Each 'run' of wagons, on balanced up and down workings, was attached by two chains. These had links as large as that of a standard link coupling at the end which was dropped over the drawhook of the leading wagon. From here the chain tapered, link by link, to a size little longer than an ordinary strong dog chain; it was wound round and

A few special passenger trains were run over the C&HP in the 1950s and early 1960s for the benefit of enthusiasts. The first was organised by the Stephenson Locomotive Society and Manchester Locomotive Society and ran on 25 April 1953. The special, headed by NLR 0–6–0Ts Nos 58860 and 58856, is seen at Middleton Top awaiting its passengers who had walked up Middleton Incline.

round the cable, the smallest link being tied by a leather thong. This involved a special railway trade classification: 'chain hanger on'.

Normally it was hard to get a ride but a programme made for the BBC worked wonders, even foolhardy wonders. Travelling up on the footplate of an old LNWR tender bound for the hamlet of Longville which was dependent on this sole supply of water, gave one cause for trepidation. Looking down at the deep catchpit for runaways laid between the tracks at the bottom, there were strong hopes that the 'chain hanger on' had made a secure job of it. Knowledge is sometimes inconveniently recalled! Such as that the pit had been placed there after a spectacular runaway in February 1888 when a brake van and a wagon of limestone had broken away at the top of the incline. After shooting through Cromford yard, beating any landspeed record of the time by a handsome margin, they took flight and in one huge leap they cleared two sidings, the Cromford canal, a farm road and the Midland main line. Peace of mind was not helped either by recalling that

166

even in the mid-1950s the motive power on the next incline was still the old Butterley Company's beam engine installed when the line was built. This ride was by courtesy of a dismantled ex-LNWR 0–6–0 DX, installed in 1884.

At the top the old Chopper shunted wagons, trundling them several times a day to Middleton Bottom where the 'Cromford Experience' was re-enacted. The Butterley engine did its job quite happily.

At Middleton, more sidings; and, in the small shed, a couple of North London tanks. Cam was quite right. One of these ancients was still in LMS livery, the other in new gas-tarred black had British Railways emblazoned across her side tanks. One still carried the NLR bell-mouthed chimney, the other a tall LNWR one, a reminder of Crewe standardisation and ownership. A strange migration of old engines to this bare, treeless, stonewalled uplands of the Peak. From here on it was pure adhesion working but what a working, two engines running flat out on the first stretch to just make it over the top, sparks flying in true North Western style, setting fire to the grass by the 1 in 14 gradient post. It was quite an occasion—and well worth coming back the next day for pictures.

Middleton Top shed in its declining years when it was home to two class J94 0–6–0STs, which replaced the NLR locomotives. No 68012 stands in the remains of the shed building which lost its roof during a gale in 1962. On the road adjacent to the shed are a number of ex-LNWR tenders which conveyed water for locomotives and domestic use to strategic points along the line. The limestone countryside made water both scarce and unsuitable for locomotive use.

24
IRELAND

THE Great Northern is a grand railway. Its timetable highlights the twice-daily crack Enterprise Express running up the coast from Dublin to Belfast and the seasonal Bundoran Express winding its way up the

The Tralee & Dingle Railway served the second most westerly railhead in Europe and were it not for the monthly cattle specials would have closed in 1947. These trains enabled the line to exist, just, for another six years by which time the locos and rolling stock were completely worn out. A double-headed empty cattle train hauled by 2–6–0Ts Nos 1T and 2T, built by the Hunslet Engine Company of Leeds in 1889, takes water at Anascaul in 1950. Both the locomotives were withdrawn in 1954.

border to the Atlantic rollers. Beyer Peacock of Manchester supplied 3-cylinder 4–4–0s for the first, and dainty inside-cylinder ones for the second. All have gleaming brass nameplates and a rich livery of sky blue and scarlet. The Enterprise Express is first and third class only, while others (apart from the one-class railcars) are still first, second and third. Typical of the attention paid to detail by the GN(I) on Saturday the Bundoran Express runs non-stop (70 minutes) from Dundalk to Clones, but on Mondays to Fridays makes a call each day at a different village to enable people to spend a few hours on the sands at the resort. The timetable also

lists dense suburban services at each end of the Dublin–Belfast line and sparse but well-organised services on remote branch lines; some call 'at certain Level Crossings on request'. One 'train' is but a single horse-drawn tram, from Fintona Junction to Fintona. Electric trams run up the Hill of Howth connecting with the Dublin suburban steam trains.

The tiny Dundalk, Newry & Greenore, built by the English London & North Western Railway to provide its Holyhead passengers with its own Irish port, is one of a number of minor systems unexpectedly surviving because it straddles the border and the two sides do not talk about the mounting losses. Included in the survival is the huge hotel and golf links at Greenore: you can lie in a cavernous bath with the window open inhaling a smell of Crewe steam, for three Victorian Webb 0–6–0 saddle tanks still keep going. Not only that, the original six-wheeled passenger stock is in daily use painted in LNWR plum and spilt milk.

The Belfast & County Down has green Baltic tanks to Bangor and 4–4–2 ones in a couple of sizes to Donaghadee. The newly nationalised lines of North and South have not yet had time to alter their liveries completely, so LMS red and Great Southern

Great Northern Railway (Ireland) three cylinder compound 4–4–0 No 83 Eagle *built by Beyer Peacock & Company of Gorton, Manchester in 1932 and withdrawn by the Ulster Transport Authority in 1960. Eagle carries a Belpaire boiler; the original was round top, and is painted in the glorious blue livery adopted by the GNR c1939.*

black/dark grey abound.

This is Ireland in 1949. One uses old railway ships to cross the Irish Sea. First class has plush dining rooms and there are a few cabins with beds and salt-water baths for a small supplement.

World War II has been over for nigh on four years but fuel restrictions have been severe until only months ago. Eire has but one commercial coal mine, its quality so poor that the stuff can only be used in power stations. Nationalisation will soon lead to rationalisation, so this is the time to have a last look at a scene which is, even now, a reminder of the good days.

There is much to attract. Derby built engines run on the former Northern Counties Committee (LMS) lines of the Six Counties (or 'Black North' as it can be called down south). Woolwich Moguls, inside-cylinder 4–4–0s, 0–6–0s and 2–4–0s, make up most

*There was never very much through working between any of
the Irish railways, but between 1950 and 1953 the GNR and
CIE collaborated in a through train between Belfast and Cork
named Enterprise—an extension of a purely GN train between
Belfast and Dublin. The down train (from Dublin) is pictured
at Amiens Street station Dublin, the GNR terminus, hauled
by ex-Great Southern Railways' three cylinder 4–6–0 No 802
Tailte. In the background is GNR articulated diesel railcar
'G' on a train to Howth. This service is now electrified and
the trains run through from Howth to Bray using the former
City of Dublin Junction platform Nos 5 to 7.*

of the motive power on the old Great Southern
system, now Coras Iompair Eireann (CIE). And the
last railway in the British Isles to have 'Great' in its
title, the Great Northern, still justifies it. It straddles
the border, dealing separately with two governments
who do not recognise each other… but in a few years
its mounting losses will make them talk together for
the first time.

Another system which is already surviving on
borrowed time because it also crosses the border is
the creaking Sligo, Leitrim & Northern Counties
Railways, whose 0–6–4 tanks are named but never
numbered. It is one of Ireland's attractive oddities
which of course include the narrow-gauge systems.
These range from serious concerns like the County
Donegal Railways, to the Tralee & Dingle, only
coming alive when it is poked, which we will return
to shortly.

Ireland is very much Ireland: class 3 roads are dirt,
cars are few, you bump along the branch over short
rails at a fastish lick in an old 'sax whaler' where the
guard is a 'grand man' in pouring rain which is a
'foine soft day now'. Below the border chocolate is
not rationed; you can actually find bananas and
cream after a huge steak and the Guinness is superb.
When the sun shines in the west the light is pure
crystal. But do not be surprised when the kid across
the aisle is sent to beg a sixpence.

To the English eye traffic outside the large towns

(which really means only Belfast and Londonderry, Dublin, Limerick and Cork) is sparse. But this is not just a sign of the times. It is a sensible part of the Irish way of life, for the largely agricultural community rarely moves beyond its village and market town. An absence of minerals makes railway freight traffic cling to this agricultural pattern. Many a station in rural areas has only one or at the most, two, train(s) in each direction daily, and arrival is something of an occasion, with news exchanged while parcels traffic is being bundled in and out of the van. Even such focal points as Mallow and Limerick Junction enjoy long spells of cloisteral quiet, broken by brief periods of frantic activity when the rare trains arrive, complete with vintage engine and heterogeneous stock, to make their elaborate inter-connections. Dublin's busiest stations, Amiens Street and Westland Row, compare naturally with London's Marylebone.

Checking the distances between stations on the major lines it becomes apparent that although a train may be booked to call at every one, the quality of the running is quite high and much better than the timetable might suggest. Low train mileage and the need for economy mean engines and stock have long

Cork Glanmire Road locomotive shed, probably in the early 1950s, when the CIE was still 100 percent steam. From left to right the locomotives are 342 class (D4) 4–4–0 No 346 built by the GSR in 1936 at Inchicore and withdrawn in 1960; 393 class (K1A) 2–6–0 No 394 (of SECR design) built by the GSR at Inchicore in 1930 with parts supplied by the Woolwich Arsenal, withdrawn in 1959; 60 class (D14) 4–4–0 No 60 built by the Great Southern & Western Railway at Inchicore in 1891 and rebuilt with Belpaire boiler in 1934, withdrawn in 1957; 101 class (J15) 0–6–0 No 241 built by the Great Southern & Western Railway at Inchicore in 1902 and retaining its original round-top boiler, withdrawn in 1957.

lives. In fact, apart from obvious LMS-built Moguls in the north, most date back to the old pre-1923 and 1925 companies. But this does not mean leaking, clanking engines in poor mechanical condition. Often, in performance and outward appearance, Irish steam puts its British counterpart to shame. Stand on the platform at Omagh and see the Great Northern's *Croagh Patrick* sweep in from Belfast like a well groomed horse, her immaculate livery reflecting in a symmetrical pattern the whorls made by the cleaner's cloth, and you cannot but be impressed. Above the magnificent coat of arms on her splasher, the brass nameplate flashes in the sun whilst cab and boiler fittings are spotless beyond reproach.

The Irish train can be equally magnificent, if comprising a motley collection of vehicles in shape, size and age. It is reminiscent of the LNWR. In fact the Great Southern has a North Western air about it, its engines all carrying Crewe-type cast number-plates. Within a decade change will become complete, today's occasional modern steel coach will be the norm, its elliptical roof and electric lighting

The London & North Western Railway owned the Dundalk, Newry & Greenore Railway in Co Louth and Co Down. It was a microcosm of the parent company. This photograph taken at Greenore about 1950 shows one of the six 0–6–0STs, No 3, which were Ramsbottom/Webb special tanks adapted for the 5ft 3in gauge and typical LNW signals. The whole system closed on 31 December 1951.

replacing the gaslit period interior of the elderly eight-wheeled clerestory or the jolting six-wheeler. The latter still populate the branches snaking along with no sprung seats and with the old pot-lamp holders still in place on the roof. These ancients, however, are well maintained and upholstered, exteriors newly painted and door handles polished. Passengers are few, in first class usually only the occasional priest.

The narrow gauge West Clare boasts a six-wheeled saloon still in Great Southern maroon with that company's coat of arms on the doors. The Donegal too has its saloons but these only come out on the occasion of the Bank Holiday steam specials to Ballyshannon.

With the exceptions of the new Ulster Transport Authority's (ex-NCC) Belfast–Londonderry, the Great Northern's Dublin–Belfast, and CIE's Dublin–Cork routes, there are few Irish lines which would not be considered to be very secondary in England, essential links though they provide. This is particularly true of the undulating single tracks that run across the Midland bogs towards the mountainous far west of Connaught or Kerry. There is an air of adventure that permeates these trains which two or three times a day set out over their long and usually lonely tracks. In his *Lines of Character*, L.T.C. Rolt calls them 'ships of the bogs' and the stations 'rare oases welcoming their coming'. Such thoughts slide easily through the mind when musing over the

journey in a well-stocked and comfortable dining car making the most of the wide loading gauge of the 5ft 3in track. On the longer branch lines in the south, one-time Great Southern & Western Class J15 0–6–0s introduced as early as 1866 vie with Midland Great Western 2–4–0s dating from 1880. Most of these lines, like the Valentia Harbour branch (the most westerly in Europe) are full of character. Virtually all such trains are mixed and slow. But who would be rushing when there is so much to enjoy? But do not take too much notice of the timetable broadsheets. Trains are worked to local advantage.

For example, the 3.06pm from Cahirciveen to Farranfore, leaves at 2.30. It gives people plenty of time to do their shopping at Killorglin. No notice of this appears of course; why should it? Dublin seems pretty nearly as remote and irrelevant as Paris so far as Kerry people are concerned.

The independent Sligo, Leitrim & Northern Counties, linking Enniskillen in the north with Sligo in the south, is a line of such decrepitude that only a personal ride over it can demonstrate. It defies adequate description. The daily mixed runs within an hour or so of time. It has one magnificent tri-composite coach. The first class seats are coming unstuffed in places, the lighting is intermittent. Yet two of the 0–6–4 tanks are modern, delivered in 1947 by Beyer Peacock notwithstanding the railway is in receivership. Investigation proves that they are being paid for on the never never. Maybe Beyer Peacock did not do a customer investigation before starting work and have not been paid? While passenger business even at the line's HQ, Manorhamilton, is light, many cattle pass through it. Handed over by CIE they are taken over by the GN (or GN(I) as it should be properly called) en route from cattle fairs in the south to the English market.

The continued independence of the lines crossing the border is fine for the enthusiast who can revel in the blue of the Great Northern, the geranium red of the County Donegal or the olive green of the Lough Swilly. The narrow-gauge railways are a fascinating group notwithstanding the Damoclesian sword which hangs over them all. They have no parallel whatever with any lines over the water. Once there were eighteen of them, all using the Irish sub-stan-dard gauge of three feet with a total mileage of 562. Now there are seven, mostly the longer concerns which were built to serve the 'congested areas', a

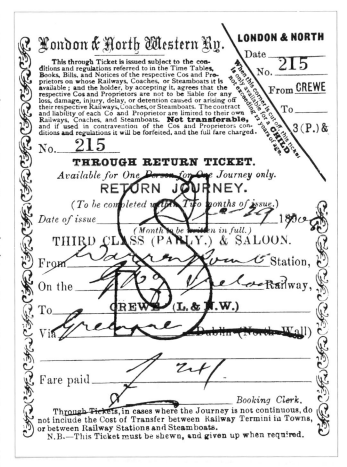

The return portion of a London & North Western Railway ticket permitting travel from Warrenpoint to Crewe via the steamer service from Greenore. Third class on the train and saloon (first class) on the boat, all for 24s (£1.20).

peculiar turn of the century phrase for the poor regions of the west with more population than resources to feed them.

The Tralee & Dingle Railway is special. Built on a shoestring to open up one of the poorest of Ireland's counties, the life of this remarkable piece of railway hangs by a very slender thread, its active locomotive power down to three 2–6–0 tanks which only come to life on the occasion of the monthly cattle fair at Dingle. On the Friday before the empty stock is worked down in one or two trains, depending on the season, returning fully loaded the following day. These trips are probably the last examples of adven-turous railroading in the British Isles; they will cease when the road becomes paved. Of all the railways of Ireland the T&D retains its original character. The rails lie rusty, dulled by a month's disuse, only three

Three of the three-foot gauge lines inherited by the Great Southern Railways lasted until the 1950s, and the West Clare until 1961. The Cavan & Leitrim main line connected the MGW at Dromod with the GNR at Belturbet and the Arigna branch from the line's headquarters at Ballinamore served Ireland's only viable coal mine. For most of its length the Arigna branch was a roadside tramway and is seen here at an ungated crossing coming alongside the road in 1957. The locomotive is ex-Tralee & Dingle 2–6–0T No 3T built by the Hunslet Engine Company of Leeds in 1889 and transferred to the C&L in 1941 and lasted until closure of the C&L in 1959. The photograph was taken in the last couple of years of the line's life.

nothing, absolutely nothing, is ever cleaned. The locos and rolling stock, however, are pieces of Irish railway history; the original C&L 4–4–0 tanks have been augmented by 2–4–2 tanks from the erstwhile Cork, Blackrock & Passage Railway where they ran nippy suburban services and *all three* classes of engines from the Tralee & Dingle, a standard 2–6–0 tank No 3T, 2–6–0 tank No 4T (the small Kerr Stuart engine) and the infamous 2–6–2 tank No 5T which was wrecked with the runaway pig train at Glengalt. Add to this lot a curious set of coaches from old bus bodies to venerable eight-wheelers having clerestories and American-type balconies with gates in veranda rails.

Further north the two largest narrow-gauge systems are thriving and retrenching respectively. Owned jointly by the Great Northern and the successors of the English Midland Railway, the County Donegal Railways Joint Committee is very much alive. The credit here is due almost entirely to the introduction of railcars by the late Henry Forbes

(pronounced 'Forbess' on the railway) between the wars. This remarkable man also introduced a system of sealed containers loaded in Dublin by the Great Northern travelling in bond through the intervening Six Counties, being transhipped at Strabane to narrow-gauge flat trucks. Ingenuity and variety have kept this hundred and one mile gem of the narrow gauge going. With its railcars, including a veteran from the long closed Clogher Valley Railway in the North, the ten geranium red 2–6–4 and 4–6–4 tanks, all named, the CDRJC has an over-abundance of power to cover its passenger and freight services. Often special vans painted red are attached to the rolling rollicking railcars giving rapid parcels facilities, but freight is usually run by steam several times daily except beyond Stranorlar to the west where once a day suffices. The solely English-owned section from Londonderry to Strabane is one hundred percent steam.

A permit to ride in the van or on the engine of the daily mixed west from Stranorlar brings pure delight. Perhaps the engine is the 4–6–4T *Erne* or the 2–6–4T *Columbkille*, but whatever the motive power the train will be long and heavy, sweeping round on a great curve to face a continuous five mile grade of 1 in 60 into the Donegal highlands, a climb which keeps the fireman busy. The crew are probably the McMenamin brothers who have been on the job almost forever. Topping the summit the tracks parallel the edge of Lough Mourne, its steel waters ever troubled by the mountain winds. The mountains ahead seem to bar any further progress but a deep and narrow defile opens up whence the train drops down through the stark Barnesmore Gap, again at 1 in 60, the track clinging to precipitous slopes high above the floor of the pass. Down through Lough Eske with a view encompassing the Blue Stack Mountains and into lavishly-signalled Donegal station for a shunt before traversing the long winding extension to the deep waters of Killybegs.

The time to visit the Donegal system is the August Bank Holiday Monday, when steam passenger trains run from Strabane and Stranorlar taking town and village to the sea at Ballyshannon—or rather Bundoran, a good walk further on. The sight of these specials using every available piece of passenger rolling stock there is, wending their way home in the dusk high above the road through the Barnesmore Gap, is etched in the memory for a lifetime.

The Donegal and Lough Swilly systems meet across the road at Letterkenny. The Swilly's story is very different. Beautifully maintained dark green 4-6-2 and 4-6-0 tanks work the freights to Letterkenny and Buncrana, each with a slatted wooden-seated passenger brake van at the end. In the shed at Pennyburn, Londonderry, two huge 4-8-4 tanks slumber and at Letterkenny there is a 4-8-0 tender engine, once used for the wild and desolate extension to Burtonport, now closed and taken up. It was seventy-four miles this journey, entailing a spectacular climb to the far west out of Derry and the crossing of the Owencarrow river by a long viaduct. In 1925 a train was blown off it.

Handfuls of passengers, mostly shoppers from Pluck or Newtoncunningham use the unwelcoming compartments of the Lough Swilly brake van on the Letterkenny–Londonderry train. These freights are well loaded and shunt nearly everywhere. There is a box of butter here, a few empty coal wagons there and often a cattle van or two full of beef which get discharged pell mell onto the station platform. The railway runs through prosperous agricultural country and a great deal of general traffic is available including tons of potatoes. Soon it will all go by road.

After Newtoncunningham the line drops down along the shores of Lough Swilly, the driver closing the regulator and wiping his hands on a piece of oily waste; he leaves the job of braking entirely to the guard, explaining that he is a 'grand man'. As the train gathers momentum, and the swaying wagons behind seem disproportionately large for the ever narrowing track ahead, one loses faith for a second

until the screw brake takes effect and couplings tighten. Tooban Junction, a desolate island platform with a lonely signal box, is the crossing place for the down goods from Derry and the jumping off point for the Buncrana branch which still sees the odd passenger excursion at weekends and Bank Holidays. The border comes next with perfunctory customs examinations, then the workshops at Pennyburn seemingly full up with company buses and the dark gloomy Graving Dock terminus. What a railway it must have been in its prime.

In the north things are more prosaic, the Great Northern and the old NCC run into Londonderry linking it with Dublin and Belfast, though off the Derry to Belfast line at Ballymoney there is a jewel, the three-foot gauge Ballycastle branch which has bogie *corridor* coaches still in LMS red and 2-4-2 Worsdell von Borries compound tanks. The coaches are leftovers from the unique narrow-gauge boat-trains from Larne to Ballymena, now but a memory. Close to Fair Head on the Antrim coast Ballycastle is a popular watering place in the summer, and seasonal traffic is heavy, so the line has not yet succumbed but

The three-foot gauge Londonderry & Lough Swilly Railway served some of the more isolated parts of Co Donegal and was effectively a main line as the remotest terminus was Burtonport, 74¼ miles from Derry. To work the train services the L&LS owned the only eight coupled narrow-gauge locomotives in Ireland, two 4-8-0 tender engines and two 4-8-4 tanks. No 6, one of the tanks built by Hudswell Clarke & Company of Leeds in 1912, is seen at Derry Pennyburn shed before the war. The railway finally closed in 1953 and No 6 lasted until closure.

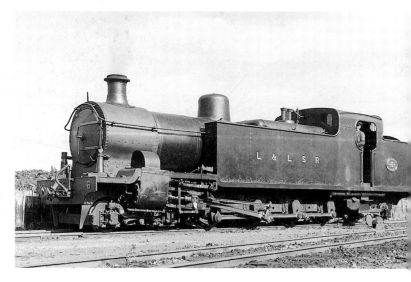

The other narrow-gauge railway serving Co Donegal was the County Donegal Railways Joint Committee, jointly owned by the Great Northern Railway (Ireland) and Midland Railway of England and its successors. The CDR also traversed some wild country especially the climb to 591ft through the Barnesmore Gap between Stranorlar, its headquarters, and Donegal town. A return excursion from Ballyshannon hauled by a 2–6–4T is seen passing through the Barnesmore Gap on 3 August 1959.

time is not a friend. Even in the more prosperous north, Ireland is Ireland and less than a decade ago, in 1943, a train of two passenger coaches, ten wagons and a van ran away on the steep gradient dropping down into Ballycastle running through the buffer stops at the terminus, ending up in a stream on the other side of the road. No one was hurt.

Belfast is dour but the home of express trains. At Great Victoria Street station there are blue engines with teak stock to run over the Great Northern where, on the Dublin route, the dining cars have two separate locked cupboards of drinks for customs purposes. At York Road the Derby Moguls and Class 2 4–4–0s of the former LMS NCC, now the Ulster Transport Authority, go to Londonderry and the coast towns of Portrush and Larne, all with somersault semaphores. Last but certainly not least—for in its array of engines are a 2–4–0, 0–6–0s and an army of tanks—is the unique Belfast & County Down at Queens Quay. This is more like home, but an Irish home for all that.

The West Clare Railway was the longest three-foot gauge line, at 53 miles, inherited by the GSR and ran from Ennis to Kilrush and Kilkee. The line was dieselised in 1953/5 with four railcars, similar to CDR Nos 19 and 20, and three 0–4–0+0–4–0 locomotives but even this could not stave off closure which came in 1961. The WCR owned a total of 16 locomotives over the years and No 3c, originally named Ennistymon, was one of the last two engines built for the WCR by the Hunslet Engine Company of Leeds in 1922 and was withdrawn in 1953. No 3c is seen taking water at Ennis in 1950. The 5ft 3in line can be seen through the bridge.

25
ANOTHER ROUTE

ONE of the great joys of exploring Britain by train was that without extra cost your return journey could be by a different and much longer route. Even today there are plenty of opportunities for stretching a bargain, like going from the West Country to Paddington the direct way and stopping off at Swindon or Bristol on the return. But it is absolutely nothing like it used to be. With few exceptions, today there is a definite route and anything else is at least out of the ordinary and much slower. Many of the trains we loved ran on parallel routes for hundreds of miles, or even took journeys that criss-crossed each other, such as at Carlisle. Who among us went to Scotland and returned the same way?

Another route. Just say those two words and the brain automatically recalls the great alternatives of yesteryear and the fun we had deciding how to make the best of our opportunities. 'Another Route' was indeed a heading

The Great Central London extension was probably more useful as a cross-country route with its connection to the Great Western via Woodford and Banbury than an alternative route to London. Ex-GCR 4–6–0 LNER class B1 (later B18, following the introduction of the Thompson design in 1942) No 5196 is seen near Rothley in August 1931 with the Ports to Ports Express–Newcastle, Barry and Swansea.

Edinburgh was served by three routes from England: East Coast, West Coast and Waverley. The latter had through trains from St Pancras to Edinburgh and the day service in BR days was named The Waverley. The down train is leaving Leeds City North (formerly Wellington) c1959 hauled by Jubilee class 4–6–0 No 45694 Bellerophon.

liberally used in what might be described as the lazy Londoner's *Bradshaw*, the monthly *ABC Alphabetical Railway Guide*. Only being of use for journeys to or from the capital, and thus for practical purposes only for Londoners, it nevertheless had a substantial circulation and generations of hotel porters and individual travellers consulted it as the easiest way of seeing what was available. For enthusiasts, it usefully cited the fares for each route, 'Fares as above' of course implying you could return by the longer way for the same money.

Undoubtedly the most fortunate were those going from London north to places like Manchester, Edinburgh and Glasgow. Not only was their diversity of route but of restaurant-car trains as different as Catholic, C of E and Methodist. And while in many cases one route was quicker, there was often not much in it and one might anyway run at less convenient times. Or did we kid ourselves that the route we wanted to use was the one whose train left just as we would be ready?

To cite a few examples, Birmingham did have two nearly equal services until the London Midland's was effectively withdrawn to make way for the West Coast main line electrification, after which the Western was a very secondary alternative. Birmingham business folk swore allegiance to Paddington or Euston, and when two of different religion wanted to travel together it was like deciding whether the Catholic would go to the Methodist harvest festival or vice versa. Only perhaps in the Glasgow area were feelings more entrenched... and there it was as much about which way to take the daily train to work as making an occasional long-distance journey. If the North Eastern Railway showed what monopoly could achieve, then Glasgow suburban services epitomised the glory of competition.

180

If you had 'done' all three routes used by through trains, the London to Manchester journey was one that called for especial deliberation. Euston might have a grand entrance but before rebuilding was a pretty miserable station to depart from, and while the train itself would be fast and comfortable the scenery was not in the top league. Marylebone was a fun place to leave from, and the fact there were fewer opportunities to take ex-Great Central rails had to be taken into account. The end of the journey was spectacular, and since the completion of the first main-line electrification in Britain the journey through the long Pennine tunnel was no longer a pain; but having to share the exit from London with London Transport *was,* and the number of through services was limited. Against that, they tended to be less crowded, but the coaches could be dirty. The restaurant car was not as good: it was here we had been put in our place. The LNER did not serve Yorkshire pudding *and* horseradish. St Pancras was ever delightful. The train would be comfortable and the restaurant car probably the best, but it would be a short train and could be crowded. Again the later part of the journey was better, the passage through the Peak District indeed being grander than anything else on any of the routes. The train made more stops, seldom if ever missing Leicester, but Derby always gave a warm glow. Now, which way would you go tomorrow if you had to make the journey and all three routes were operating? For the writer it would have to be St Pancras.

For most railway lovers it would undoubtedly be St Pancras for Edinburgh or Glasgow, simply because that has been impossible for so many years. When everything was still open and running, the choice was not so obvious, for while you would never waste a passage of the Long Drag over the Settle & Carlisle reading, the extra time was very considerable. You could indeed only do the journey sensibly by the one daily through train each to Edinburgh (The Waverley) or Glasgow (The Thames–Clyde Express). But hold on; what is the hurry? Why not break the journey at Leeds… but then if you went from King's Cross you could do so at York, or if from Euston at Preston and take that promised visit to Blackpool. The choice was endless, and it came back to personal preference or your railway religion. We just count ourselves lucky we could take each route in turn, enjoying Shap and Beattock, the Pennines and the Long Drag, the cathedrals and East Coast.

There was nothing to stop you mixing and matching your own route. Glasgow St Enoch to Carlisle by the Glasgow & South Western line through

An excess ticket for the alternative route. Travel from Glasgow to Nuneaton via Leeds, instead of Crewe, cost this National Serviceman four shillings (20p) extra in 1959.

The LNER inherited two routes from London to Cambridge, one ex-Great Eastern from Liverpool Street and the other ex-Great Northern from King's Cross. The latter was probably the more popular and was served by express trains, some with buffet cars. Class 16/2 No 8787, one of the 'Royal Clauds' is passing Marshmoor with an up Cambridge on 25 May 1937. The stock appears to be five GN corridors with a non-corridor bringing up the rear but no buffet.

Above *The Midland & South Western Junction Railway was a cross-country line from Cheltenham (Lansdown) MR to Andover Junction LSWR and on over the LSWR to Southampton which fell into the GWR net in 1923. There were never any very fast trains this way but it provided a useful link, and between the wars there was a through coach from Liverpool to Southampton which was detached from the Pines Express at Cheltenham. In this view an ordinary passenger train from Andover to Cheltenham is leaving Cirencester Watermoor on 25 May 1953. GWR 4300 class 2–6–0 No 6384 is in charge.*

some of Scotland's finest non-barren scenery, to be savoured on a summer's evening after the LMS twelve-wheeler tea car came on at ugly Kilmarnock, and then south by the West Coast main line since it would be too dark to enjoy the Long Drag. But then through trains, especially sleepers serving Paisley, also performed that trick.

Cambridge was another place that had you alternating between routes, though generally the ambience of the buffet car expresses from King's Cross won. As for a journey between Cambridge and Oxford, the choice was between not doing it at all, finding an excuse to do it via London or somewhere else, or treat the wretched direct train as a joke. The Somerset & Dorset was altogether more businesslike than the link between the two great seats of learning. Many S&D journeys could of course equally well be taken via Southampton, but we loved the Joint Line and revelled in the fact that if you bought a ticket from Bridgwater to Paddington you could return from Waterloo via Templecombe… and occasionally save a minute or two on Western timings.

Sometimes we went from Marylebone out of homage to those who had put their faith in the Great Central, for here was a railway that hardly provided any journeys that could not be done equally well by another line. Faith indeed! We wondered what the hotel was like across the street at Marylebone when it welcomed the first passengers at the turn of the century, and despised the fact that, badly run down, it was now BR's headquarters. 222 Marylebone Road was a hateful address, for while much of BR was super, the overall policy was and became ever less attractive, culminating in Beeching's wretched 1963 report. The enquiry before the report had but one touch of joy: branch line closures were halted while it leisurely took place.

The Midland was one of three routes, all with through trains, between London and Manchester. It was also the most scenic as it traversed the heart of the Peak District. Jubilee class 4–6–0 No 45598 Basutoland awaits the right away with the 4.00pm Derby to St Pancras express in June 1955.

Opposite below *The Cheshire Lines Committee provided two alternative routes from Manchester, one to Chester and the other to Liverpool. A special empty coaching stock train is passing Knutsford c1949 hauled by LNER class J10 0–6–0 No 65161. All the CLC's passenger stock was non-corridor although some had internal lavatories.*

Great Western locomotives usually worked the West to North trains south of Hereford and/or Shrewsbury and Grange class 4–6–0 No 6861 Crynant Grange *is passing Abergavenny Junction with a northbound train in September 1952. Alongside the goods shed is an ex-LNWR 0–8–0 No 49168 fitted with tender cab for working the line to Merthyr.*

Opposite below The LMS had *an alternative route from London to Swansea via Stafford, Shrewsbury and Llandrindod Wells (Central Wales line) at the same fare as the direct route from Paddington. This anomaly was abolished with the rationalisation of fares in 1952. There was, and still is, a service from Shrewsbury to Swansea, and an ordinary passenger train from Shrewsbury is seen at Builth Road High Level, where the Central Wales crossed the Cambrian's Mid-Wales line from Moat Lane to Brecon. The locomotive is BR class 5 4–6–0 No 73025 allocated to Shrewsbury when that depot was coded 89A (1961–3).*

The era of the trains we loved ended along with many of their routes, certainly 'Another Route', with Beeching—the Great Central of course being a main casualty.

Glasgow to Edinburgh, Manchester to Leeds, Cardiff to Birmingham, London to Canterbury: we were not short of journeys where the choice could be sensibly made either way. But in practical terms one of the biggest choices was slightly different: whether to go cross-country or via London. From the West to Scotland that might involve leaving only an hour earlier for the same arrival time, and the exhilaration of a fast trip to and from the capital in exchange for the undoubted delights of a cross-country West to North service (still via Hereford and picturesque Ludlow of course) but the dubious pleasure of being shunted away from a platform during the Crewe stopover. If we were interested in locomotive performance, accelerations of the crack trains to the capital began to sway things, and soon the cross-countries were anyway a dying breed. You could no longer get from Devon to Folkestone with a single change at Reading (and that after arriving there by slip coach), and East Anglia lost most of its through services, including the restaurant car train that had taken the Joint line to Yarmouth and the Edinburgh–Cambridge service.

Cross-country trains had entirely their own aura. Few had the most recent rolling stock, and most stopped at all major traffic points where a considerable proportion of the passengers changed. It sometimes seemed that only you and the restaurant car crew remained the same. Many of these through trains had run at the same time for decades, being skilfully interwoven with services to or from London on successive routes to the capital.

But so had many branch-line services, and we must not forget that some journeys might involve taking a succession of all-station locals. One difficulty was discovering whether a return ticket was valid by our chosen deviation, as from Bristol to Aberystwyth out via Brecon and back via Carmarthen. If we could not do it by Monthly Return, the standard one-and-a-third times single rate, then there was always the Circular Ticket. That meant going to the local booking office and asking for a bespoke tour,

Above *South West and South Wales to North West trains were routed via the Severn Tunnel (from the South West) and Newport (from South Wales) then on to Hereford and Shrewsbury, the various portions joining at Pontypool Road. Here one such train, composed of a mixture of LMS and GW stock hauled by GW County class 4–6–0 No 1003* County of Wilts, *is seen near Llantilo Pertholey about one mile north of Abergavenny Junction on 11 September 1952.*

Above Brecon *was a jointly owned station and was served by four different railways, the Cambrian, Brecon & Merthyr, Neath & Brecon and Midland, prior to 1922. For many years the Midland worked the passenger trains over the Neath & Brecon to Colbren Junction which ran through from Hereford to Swansea St Thomas, providing an alternative route from Birmingham. The 6.20pm train for Neath (Riverside) on 9 August 1960 hauled by 5700 class 0–6–0PT No 9627 is about to depart.*

subject to an attractive discount. You had to give three days' notice. But then such journeys were usually planned over weeks if not months. The only problem was that if they were to happen near the beginning of the summer or winter timetable, you had no way of knowing whether traditional connections would continue to be maintained. In Ireland they seemed to insist on selling you tickets by routes that proved impractical and you were forever having an argument with one of the ticket collectors who seemed to appear with great regularity out of the bogs.

One other aspect of another route needs to be mentioned: the railway hotels. Mainly adjuncts to larger stations, they were railway institutions in their own right, in the days we are talking about almost invariably the best (outside London). Arriving in Glasgow by three different routes from England meant you could savour the delights of the showpieces of three former railways without going into the street.

26
INVERNESS–EUSTON

IF there is a single platform in the provinces that has seen greater drama than any other, it must surely be the longest, curved one at Inverness, No 2. That is where our Royal Highlander for London, a sitting, eating and sleeping train, waits while the sun is still high in the sky on a late August evening in 1959. We feel our own touch of drama as we check not only for our own but others' names on the lists of sleeping car berth allocations posted at the platform head. There is ours sandwiched between household names travelling second like us, though first class has a higher proportion of Honourables, Lords and Right Honourables.

As we walk two-thirds of the length of the platform to check in and deposit our baggage in our LMS two-berth sleeper, two Black Fives back onto the train… and we think of what has used this platform in bygone times. Always first to come to mind are those 'caravan trains' of pre-Grouping days, monstrous processions of carriages of many English and Scottish railways, each displaying a distinctive livery, along with a motley assortment of horse boxes and other four-wheeled conveyances of livestock and road carriages. Traditionally they arrived for the beginning of the grouse season on the Glorious Twelfth and departed two or three weeks later when the aristocracy had shot their quota of birds. On impulse we walk to the front van, and are not disappointed. Grouse addressed to the Claridge's and other top hotels and restaurants make you feel you are part of history… and there is a first-class passenger taking a brace into his twelve-wheeled LMS sleeper.

A lot of other history has been enacted on platform 2. For example, during two World Wars enormous contingents of military and naval people arrived and departed here, and we think of the heroic efforts made to keep exceptionally heavy traffic moving, especially by the Highland Railway in the 1914–18 war when the navy was based in the far north.

Our luggage in the sleeping compartment, we now claim our two window seats in a Mark 1 BR coach with superior wood fittings, but pause only momentarily to leave some personal belongings on the seat and move to our third position, in the restaurant car. 'First sitting', we are told forcibly, unable to determine whether second has sold out or the staff just insist on everyone eating early unless there is a genuine overflow. 'Take your seats on departure.'

Rather than return to our compartment (or sleeper) for the final ten minutes we walk around the romantic station, built on two sides of a triangle, the Rose Street curve completing it. When we arrived a couple of weeks ago, our train shot north along the curve and backed into this Templecombe of the North, supposedly to allow cross-platform connections to Wick/Thurso and Kyle of Lochalsh. Though, as we shall see, our train

Opposite below During the summer many trains for Bournemouth were routed from the LMS system onto the Somerset & Dorset at Bath. Single line sections and the steep climb over the Mendips, requiring many trains to be double headed, gave the line a unique operational character. Here an up train from Bournemouth tackles the steep climb to Masbury summit at Winsor Hill with two S&D locomotives in charge on 23 August 1952. Class 7F 2–8–0 No 53802 (S&D No 82) leads the way with class 4F 0–6–0 No 44559 (S&D No 59) behind. Note the S&D passenger train headcode.

supports a whole network of connections, passengers from the far North for the Royal Highlander would have arrived long ago, at 2.38pm, just after those from Kyle of Lochalsh. No doubt they have enjoyed afternoon tea in that Highland Railway showpiece, the Station Hotel. The evening trains from the North connect with the 'midnight', which has sleepers from Inverness to Edinburgh (recently introduced) and Glasgow—and even a through coach from Wick to Glasgow.

Not that the station is dull right now. Over on the far side at platform 7 is the last of the three daily departures for Kyle, due to leave at the same moment as us, while at platform 6 a small crowd is waiting to greet relatives and friends off the 10.00am from Glasgow, which is going to back in. At platform 3 the 6.00pm semi-fast to Aberdeen is beginning to load. Inverness has always enjoyed rush hours like this between long siestas, though even then the booking office is busy with people arranging the most complicated of journeys. The station's fascination is increased by the fact that most passengers are making journeys of several hours, some like ourselves of well over half a day. Yet the coat of arms of the Inverness & Nairn shows that the Highland capital's first railway was a purely local, self-contained affair.

Neither we nor the Kyle train leave at 5.40pm, for at 5.41, six minutes late, the 10.00 from Glasgow takes the Rose Street curve. It has not started to back in, to give a connection for Kyle, before we are given right away, and set off along the Firth under the magnificent signal gantries. Not so long ago the Euston sleeper started even earlier, a recent improvement being the introduction of an all-stations local to Aviemore, which allows us to run there non-stop.

Our Black Fives are allowed 62 minutes for the $34\frac{3}{4}$ miles mainly of hard climbing—a vast improvement on the last century when everything went via Forres. But the original road is still taken on Sundays and other days there is still a through section that way which we will pick up at Aviemore. It has a first- but no longer a second-class sleeper. We indeed saw it leave at 3.55pm at the back of an Aberdeen train. The through coaches are then scheduled to spend 30 minutes in Forres before being taken by a stopper to Aviemore, usually behind a 'Caley Bennie'; a number of these ex-Caledonian 4–4–0s, the equivalent to the ex-Highland Bens, are allocated to both Forres and Aviemore. But Black Fives are pretty ubiquitous on the Carr Bridge line and indeed services north from Inverness. The Black Fives are nicknamed Hikers by Highland enginemen. The nickname was presumably transferred from the ex-Great Eastern's B12s used on the Great North of Scotland section of the LNER and from the start were regular visitors to Inverness before Stanier introduced his 5P5Fs. For their respective railways, they were the first 4–6–0s imported from England to the Highlands.

So into the restaurant car for our four-course *table d'hôte* dinner, adequate but not as good as we are used to on the Western.

Occasionally the steam and smoke driven by an easterly breeze block our vision, but we make full use of the restaurant car's picture windows to soak in the scenery slowly passing by. A view of the Moray Firth and the whole Inverness area opens up as we climb up the 'new' line, and catch a glimpse of the prehistoric Clava Cairns from the viaduct. Bleak Culloden Moor and then rugged mountains. On the sharp curves we alternately see the Black

Fives toiling away and the train's rear.

We do not see another train till reaching Aviemore, but here there seems to be a gala display of activity, with several locomotives on shed, the first part of our train with its first-class sleeper at the other face of the island platform waiting to be joined to us, and clearly an important down arrival expected—which rolls in two minutes early with another pair of Black Fives on its way from Perth to Inverness. The main restaurant portion goes the direct route while three coaches are detached to run via Forres, taking an extra seventy minutes to Inverness, the Caley Bennie we saw on the turntable perhaps going to take charge. We note that the Perth train has already shed one section, at Ballinluig for Aberfeldy. A short goods train has a single Black Five waiting to follow us. There is life aplenty in the Highlands, but soon the diesels will be coming and it will all change.

We are allowed fifteen minutes at Aviemore but leave a few late. The two Black Fives however seem determined to make light work of the load that has been increased to sixteen bogies, a snake that will be watched by a high proportion of the not very many people living along the next section of route of glorious scenery beside loch, through gaps in the mountains and ultimately a gorge before the summit is reached. Now we stop almost everywhere, picking up two or three people at Kincraig, Kingussie, Newtonmore, Dalwhinnie with its distillery, but miss Struan though we note it is important enough to be a starting point for a morning train to Perth. We of course stop at Blair Atholl, starting point for three services to Perth already dieselised, and at Pitlochry by which time it is dark.

Long back in our compartment, we have stayed up hoping to catch a glimpse of the Pass of Killiecrankie, but fail. So feeling a little conspicuous, we say good night to our envious companions who will sit all the way to Euston (no doubt making good use of our vacated seats) and also to our sleeping car attendant and 'retire' for the night. Or at least that was the intention, but before we have undressed we stop at Dunkeld & Birnam ('Stops on notice to take up for England', says our timetable; the solitary gent must feel important halting us) and are still not settled when nearly half an hour later, a few minutes early, we roll into Perth. In truth we have been reading a collection of excursion and other leaflets taken from Inverness booking office and dipping into the timetable, noting that with the improvements of the last few years there are now a dozen named Anglo-Scottish expresses. Those running within Scotland include the Fife Coast Express from Glasgow to St Andrews as well as the Granite City, the Saint Mungo and the Bon Accord on the Glasgow–Aberdeen run.

Having told our steward that we will not want a breakfast tray, the spirit of adventure overcomes us and we change our mind. After an early dinner it is going to be a long night, and we notice that passengers joining up to Perth can order breakfast to be delivered after Rugby. We even buy a bar of Nestlé's milk chocolate which we nibble while the restaurant car goes off. It will do breakfast service on the return working in the morning. Then to the spacious toilets also being visited by a few others off the train, regular passengers who obviously know what is best. Perth's own sleeper (that involved in the Harrow & Wealdstone disaster) has already left, but we see a local in from Dundee Tay Bridge and what seem to be endless shunting movements. Again we leave late, catching a glimpse of the 8.15pm diesel from Glasgow Buchanan Street to Dundee. It is still two and a half hours before the 1.25 restaurant car from Euston to Perth arrives, running most of the way behind the mid-day Scot which will have picked up a through Glasgow coach from Plymouth. The more you learn and remember, the more you want to consult your timetable: it is called compulsion. Constantly one has to remember the Scottish Region arranges tables outward from Glasgow and Edinburgh first and then to them, so first comes Glasgow to Carlisle.

We wish it were daylight to enjoy the complications of the Stirling to Motherwell main line, and certainly we wonder why we as well as Perth's own sleeper stop at Coatbridge (Central), apparently an important traffic point. But by now we are dozing off, if not deeply asleep.

We just regain consciousness at Carlisle and Crewe, more on account of snippets of conversation from the porters pushing barrows than the actual stop. Nuneaton (Trent Valley) we miss entirely, but a couple from a neighbouring cabin decide it is time we were all awake as they chirp away in the corridor on the approach to Rugby, and we hear that familiar sleeping car sound coming from the pantry at the coach's end, the tinkling of teacups being laid out. Half an hour later our breakfast tray appears; we eat it and still wish there were a restaurant car to go to for another!

We have been running fast much of the night, but now engineering work and no doubt other trains running out of sequence cause a series of delays and we see several trains carrying workers to London overtake us on the slow line while we stop and start on the fast. Maybe they are allowing some of the locals onto the main line ahead of us, the circumstance that led to the Perth sleeper crash at Harrow & Wealdstone. But this morning is bright and there is no fear of our driver passing signals. Indeed, he seems to slam on the brake at the first sight of a distant at caution.

And so we drop down the bank and through the tunnels into Euston, fifteen minutes late at 8.50am, 15 hours 10 minutes after leaving Inverness. It has indeed been a long, hungry night but at least we caught some sleep lying down and are surprised at how sprightly the majority who have sat up all night walk along the platform.

Auto-Train Appeal

Among the trains we most loved were the push-pull auto-car ones that mainly ran on branch lines and had a culture entirely of their own. None yet runs in preservation but as Patron of the South Devon Railway Association I am appealing for funds to restore GWR 0–4–2T No 1420 and an auto-car with working push-pull equipment. If you have fond memories of the Trains We Loved, please send a donation: David St John Thomas, Patron's Auto-Train Fund, South Devon Railway Association, Buckfastleigh Station, Buckfastleigh, South Devon.

DStJT

INDEX

Aberdeen, 94, 149, 152, 156, 188, 189
Aberystwyth, 30, 184
Accidents, 28, 81, 82, 92, 163, 174;
   Abermule, 88; Harrow & Wealdstone, 82,
   163, 189, 190
Adams radial tanks, *50*
Anderson, Bill, 157
Arigna branch, 174, *176*
Ashchurch, *82*
Atherstone, *123*
Atlantics, 8B 'Jersey Lily', *146*; Z, *146*, 147
Auto-cars, 112, 126
Automatic Train Control, 27, 163
Aviemore, 188, 189

B1 4–6–0 *Strang Steel, 154–5*
Badminton, *20*
Ballinamore, 174, *176*
Ballycastle line, 177, 178
Baltic tanks, 169
Banks, 42, 48, 112; Beattock, *78*, 142, *158*,
   181; Campden, *17, 21*; Dainton, *25*, 109,
   113; Gelnagalt, 174; Goodrington Sands,
   29; Gravelly Hill, 49; Hatton, *6*;
   Hemerdon, 109; Hopton, 164; Wellington,
   109
Bar/tavern cars, 93, 140
Barnard Castle, *131*
Barnesmore Gap, 177, *178*
Basingstoke, *62*, 116
Belfast, 168, 178; Great Victoria Street, *178*;
   Queen's Quay, 178; York Road, 178; –
   Cork, 170; – Londonderry, 172, 177, 178;
   & County Down Railway, 169, 178
Belturbet, 174, 176
Bennett, Arnold, 69
Birkenhead, 30, 88–9, 116
Birmingham, 30, 32, 69, 116, 126, 132, 180;
   New Street, *7, 10–11*, 12, *14*, 42, *43*, 47,
   49, 69, *73*, 83, 99; Snow Hill, *6*, 12, 30,
   69, *71*, 99, 116, 127; – Bristol, 12, *18*; –
   Glasgow, *78*; – Penzance, 12; suburban
   services, 42–52, *44, 45, 49*
Black Five 4–6–0s, *10–11*, 90, 119, 126, 187
Blackpool, 79, 82, *118*, 120, 132, 181
Boat trains, *22*, 35, 53, *57*, 60, 61, 101, 120,
   149, 177–8; Golden Arrow, 9, 59, 61;
   Night Ferry, 61
Bon Accord, 189
Bookstalls, 66–7, 69
Bournemouth, 61, 116, 132; Belle, *17*, 61, *62*
BR, 12, 16, 18, 21, 26, 27, 101, 116, 118,
   120, 123, 129, 145, 152, 157, 160, 167,
   183
Bradford, 12, 37, 116, 132
Brakes, 13, 27, 30, 64, 152, 160
Branch lines, 13, 16, 34–5, 82, 94, 111–17,
   130–3, *131*, 135, 153, 157, 169, 173, 174,
   184 *see also individual entries*
Brecon, 184, *186*; & Merthyr Railway, 186
Brighton, 56, 116; Belle, 22, 61
Bristol, 12, 109, 179, 184; Parkway, 23;
   Temple Meads, *2*, 74; & Exeter Railway,
   109
Bristolian, *2*
Broadsman, 101
Buchan line, 35, 156
Buffet cars, 24, 70, 101, 181, 183
Bulleid, Oliver, 24, 60 *see also* Pacifics
Bundoran, 177; Express, 168
Burton-on-Trent, 116, 126

Caledonian Railway, 148, 149, 152 3
Callander & Oban Railway, 153
Cambrian Coast, 87; Express, 6, *121*;
   Railway, 88, 90, 186
Cambridge, 101, 181, 183, 184; – Oxford,
   183
Camwell, Arthur, 164, 167
Cardiff, – Birmingham, 104, – Plymouth, *23*
Carlisle, 79, 152, 179, 181, 190, – Newcastle,
   152; – Stranraer, 152
Car carriers, 116, 133, 152
'Caravan trains', 187
Carmarthen, 81, 184
Castle 4–6–0s, 25, 27, 30, 90, 99; *Beaufort, 2*;
   Cardigan, 39; Carew, 112; Clun, 106–7;
   *Lamphey (Sir Edward Elgar), 126; Lydford,
   65; Monmouth, 17; Neath Abbey, 113*;
   Sudeley, 121; Swordfish, 23; Tenby, 99;
   Thornbury, 25, 110, *110*
Catch pits, *164*, 166
Cathcart Circle, 143
Cattle trains, 32, 56, 69, *161*, 162, 168, *168*,
   173–4, 177
Cavan & Leitrim Railway, 174, 176
Charing Cross 40, 60
Cheltenham, 27, 99, 182
Chester, 88, 89, 183
Children, 32, 38–41, 85, 141
Chipping Norton, *27*
Circus trains, 41
Class 5 2–6–0s, *87*, *125*; 4–6–0s, *80*, 85, 86,
   185, 188
Cleanliness, 22, 31, 81, 82, 141, 145
Clogher Valley Railway, 176
Closures, 13, 82, 100, 104, 163; Beeching,
   16, 59, 152, 183–4
Coaches, 21–4, 30, 86, 172, 176; 'concertina'
   corridor, *84*; Mark Is, *25, 99, 123*, 187,
   IIIs, *19, 77*; non-corridor, 60, 74, 76, 82,
   86, *87*, 112, 114, 135, 183; saloons, 172;
   slip, 13; with balconies, 176
Coal trains, 35–6, 79, 94, 125, 134, 149
Commuter traffic, 34, 36, 45, 53, 56, 94, 96,
   149
Compound 4–4–0s, 43, 47; *Eagle*, 169
Coras Iompair Eireann (CIE), 170, 174
Cork, Blackrock & Passage Railway, 176
Coronation, 20; Scot, *19*, 20, 149
Cornishman, 12–13, 25, 27, *99*, 101, 105,
   106–7, 109, 112
County 4–6–0s, *Somerset, 84; Wilts, 185*
County Donegal Railways, 170, 172, 173,
   176–8 *passim*
Coventry, 79, 87
Crewe, 72, 83, 89, 126, 184, 190
Croagh Patrick, 172
Cromford & High Peak Railway, 164–7
Cross-country services, *23*, 27, 32, 34, 116,
   132, 152, 179, 182, 184 *see also individual
   entries*

D49/2 4–4–0 *Albrighton, 74*
Darlington, 132, *146*
Dawlish, 101, *102–3*, 105, 120
Delays, 32, 41, 48–9, 70, 72, 74–6, 86, 120,
   190
Deltics, 24, 100, 104, 128, 133–4, 152; *Green
   Howards, 104*
Depots *see* Sheds
Derby, 79, *125*, 126–7, 181; – St Pancras, *183*
Devon Belle, *61*
Devonian, 37, 132

Diesels/dieselisation, 28, 30–1, 61, 62, *79*, 83,
   100, 128, *129*, 132, 134, 152, 189; *Cossack,
   41; Sir Edward Elgar*, 31
Director 4–4–0 *Somme*, 127
Diversions, 86–7, 132
Docks, 100, 101, 134; Immingham, 101, 104;
   Tyne, *130*
Double-heading, 53, 79, 118, 164, 174
Dover, 9, *22*, 133
Dromod, 174, 176
Drummond, Dugald, 51
Drummond T9 4–4–0s (Greyhounds), *51*, 53
Dublin, 168, 176, 177; Amiens Street, *170*,
   171; Area Rapid Transit (DART), 174;
   Westland Row, 171; – Belfast, 168–70,
   172; – Cork, 172
'Dukedog' 4–4–0s, 16, ;90
Dudley, *126*
Dundalk, Newry & Greenore Railway, 169,
   172

East Anglia, 24, 94, *95*, 97, 100, 101, 161,
   184; Region, 100
East Coast main line, 83, *95*, 97, *98*, 100,
   104, 128, 133, 145, 147, 152
Eastern Region, 100, 101, 104
Edinburgh, 134, 148, 149, 152, 156, 180;
   Princes Street, 148; Waverley, 68, *144*, 149,
   152; – Cambridge, 184; – King's Cross,
   129, 133, *145*, *156*, 181
Electrification, 12, 53, 56, 57, 83, 100, 148,
   152, 180, 181
Elizabethan, 68, 133, *133*, *145*
Elliot, John, 60
Ellis, Hamilton, 9, 16
Enniskillen, 173, 174, *178*
Euston, 34, 79, 80, 82, 83, 86, 88, *139*, 190; –
   Birmingham, 86, 180; – Glasgow, 12, *19*,
   81, 181; – Manchester, 12, *77*, *147*, 181;
   – Wolverhampton, *10–11*, 21
Excursions, 12, *14*, *39*, 60, 72, 74, 82, 85, *87*,
   96, 123, 156, 152, 177, *178*
Exeter, 60, 133; St David's, *26*, 60, 70, 109,
   112, 117; St Thomas, 120
Expresses, 22–3, 69–70, 81, 83, 96–7, 100,
   123, 132, 151; Anglo-Scottish, 69, *78*, 134,
   149, 189, 'Goods', *158*; Atlantic Coast, 57,
   60, 61; Cornish Riviera, 61, 70, 101,
   105–14; Emerald Isle, 123; Enterprise,
   168, *170*; Fife Coast, 189; Lakes, 120;
   North Atlantic, 174; Pines, *71*, 182; Ports
   to Ports, 27, 132, *179*; 'Royal Clauds', *181*;
   Thames–Clyde, 132, 149, 152, 181;
   Torbay, 70, 101; West to North, 90

Fares, 24, 48, 85, 96, 180, 184, 186; supple-
   mentary, 94
Filey, 116, 132, 133
Fish trains, 35, 94, 133, 156
Flower trains, 84–5
Flying Scotsman, 70, 94, 129, 130, 132
Forbes, Henry, 176
Forres, 188, 189
Freight traffic, 12, 16, 33, 35–6, 44, 61, 84,
   93–4, 96, 100, 133, 149, 157, 159–62,
   171, 176, *see also individual entries*; trains,
   28, 30, *30*, *82, 83*, 94, 96, 96, *111*, 126,
   127, 137, *142*, 152, 157–60, *161*, 177,
   'Cauliflower' 0–6–0s, 47, *122*, Dean, *160*,
   162, pick-up, 13, 126, 152, 'Scotch', *158*,
   159, Super D 0–8–0s, 90, 123, *124*
Fruit/vegetable trains, 35, 84, 120, 161, 177

Gas Turbine locomotive, 160
Gateshead, 98, 133–4
Glasgow, 12, 81, 132, 142–9, 152, 156, 180,
   181, 186; Buchanan Street, 149; Central,
   66, 142–3, 145, *149*; Queen Street, 148; St
   Enoch, 148–9, 152, 181; Subway, 148;
   – Aberdeen, 152, 189, – Carlisle, *190*;
   – Edinburgh, 181; Oban, 142, 149, 152;
   – Plymouth, 119; St Andrews, 189; &
   South Western Railway, 149, 152, 181
Gourock, 149; express, 143
Grand, Keith, 26
Grantham, 70, 98
Grange 4–6–0 *Crynant, 184*
Granite City, 189
Great Central Railway, 79, 94, 100, 126, 132,
   145, 179, 183–4
Great Eastern Railway (Jazz service), 94, 100,
   188
Great North of Scotland Railway, 149, 153,
   156, 188
Great Northern Railway, 94, 100, 159;
   (Ireland), 168, 169, 172–4, 176–8, *passim*
Great Southern Railway, 170–2 *passim*; &
   Western, 171, 173
Great Western Railway, 7, 19, 25–31, 57, 61,
   66, 70, 74, 88–90, 100, 115, 121, 135,
   145, 179, 182
Gresley, Sir Nigel, 96, 97 *see also* Pacifics
Greenore, 169, *172*
Grouping, 9, 12, 19, 79–80, 94, 129, 149

Halts, 31, 82; Watergate, 56
Hall 4–6–0s, 90; *Acton Burnell, 71; Berrington,
   33; Croxteth, 89*
Haulage, atmospheric, 105, 112; chain,
   165–7; horse, 169, 174
Hawkins, Philip, 13
Hayling Island line, 52
Heating, 36, 157
Heart of Midlothian, 132
Hereford, 88, 90, 184–6 *passim*
High Speed 125s, 104, 109
Highland Railway, 187
Holiday traffic, 12, *14*, 16, *29*, 33–5, 53, 54–5,
   60, *63*, 72, 85–7, 97, 101–16, *102–3*,
   106–7, *112*, *129*, 177
Holyhead, 78, 132, 169
Honeymooners, 37
Hotels, 78, 81, 142, 148, 183, 186, 188
Hull, 101, 116, 130

Inclines, 13, 160, 164–6, *164*; Lickey, *83*, 119
InterCity, 80, 83, 120
Intermediate 2–4–0s, *95*
Inverness, 133, 156, 187–8; – Euston,
   187–90; & Nairn Railway, 188
Ireland, 120, 132, 162, 168–78, 186
Isles of Scilly, 84, 116

Jubilee 4–6–0s, 9, 89; *Atlas, 123; Basutoland,
   183; Bellerophon, 180; Novelty, 21*;
   Polyphemus, 10–11; Trafalgar, 14
Jumbo 2–4–0s, 47
Junctions, 66, 83, 91, 108; Abergavenny, *184*;
   Barmouth, *15*; Buttington, 88, 90; Cairnie,
   153; Church Road, 42, 43; Cogload, 109;
   Colbren, 186; Colwich, *122*; Corianlarich,
   152–3; Cowley Bridge, 109; Evercreech,
   54–5; Ferryhill, *143*; Fintona, 169, 174;
   Halwill, *51*, 56; Harborne, 48, Hatton
   North, 99; Killin, 153; Limerick, 171,

Moyasta, 174; Pontsticill, 28; Rolleston, 163; Thingley, 26, 84, 160; Tiverton, 109; Tooban, 177; Tyseley, 99, 109; Wortley, 131

K2 2-6-0 Loch Rannoch, 153
King 4-6-0s, 25, 26, 30, 89, 108; Edward II, 102-3; George V, 26; Henry III, 113; James I, 108; James II, 6; Richard III, 6
King's Cross, 12, 12, 24, 86, 93, 94, 100, 101, 150-1, 158; – Cambridge, 101, 181, 181, 183; – Edinburgh, 104, 129, 132, 133, 145, 156, 181; – Glasgow, 12, 132; – Leeds and Bradford, 12
King's Norton, 45
Kingswear branch, 13, 29, 109
Kirkby Stephen, 116, 134
Kitchen cars, 34, 141
Knowle & Dorridge, 99
Kyle of Lochalsh, 187, 188

Lake District, 79, 82
Lancashire & Yorkshire Railway, 79, 83
Leeds, 12, 116, 130, 132, 180, 181
Leicester, 66, 69, 126, 181
Level crossings, 61, 70, 134, 169
Liveries, 26, 30-1, 79, 83, 100, 112, 118, 121, 145, 169, 173
Liverpool, 24, 60, 79, 116, 183; – Southampton, 182
Liverpool Street, 24, 67, 94, 96, 100, 101, 104, 162; – Cambridge, 181; – Norwich, 101
LMS, 20, 30, 34, 45, 77-82, 96, 138, 141, 149, 152, 174
LNER, 20, 66, 94-7, 95, 98, 100, 129, 130, 149, 152, 159, 181, 188
LNWR, 45-8, 79, 83, 147, 165, 169, 172
London, 23, 61, 70, 74, 81, 134, 180, 184 see also individual termini; – Barrow–Workington, 122; – Canterbury, 184; – Manchester, 181, 183; – Swansea, 184; – Brighton, & South Coast Railway, 53, 56; – Midland Region, 82-3, 116; – & North Western Railway, 50, 56, 182; North – Railway, 164, 167
Londonderry, 172, 174, 176-8, & Enniskillen Railway, 174, 175; & Lough Swilly Railway, 173, 177
Lord Nelson 4-6-0 Howard of Effingham, 22
Luggage, 23; PLA, 13, 32, 40, 85, 119, 137
Lyme Regis branch, 50

Machines, automatic, 67, 89
Mail trains, 32-3, 143, 152; TPOs, 13, 32
Management, 56, 57, 60, 80, 96-7, 100, 132
Manchester, 12, 79, 83, 94, 96, 112, 116, 126, 180, 181, 183, – Chichester, 183; – Leeds, 184; – Liverpool, 183; – Paignton, 112
Mancunian, 77, 123
Manor 4-6-0s, 4, 16, 90, 119, Foxcote, 15, Fritwell, 136
Maps, 66, 132, 156
Marylebone, 83, 94, 132, 145, 171, 183; – Edinburgh, 152; – Manchester, 12, 96, 181
Maunsel, R.E.L., 63
Mayflower, 26, 101
Meals, 24, 34, 70, 101, 112, 119, 138-41, 156, 188; breakfast, 22, 138-40 passim, 189, 190; coffee, 24, 38, 139; dinner, 101, 188; tea, 112, 138-40 passim
Merchant Venturer, 160
Middleton Top, 164-7, 166
Midland, 18, 77, 79, 178, 180, 183, 186; & Great Northern, 104, 116; & Great Western, 14, 173; & South Western Junction, 182
Midlander, 10-11, 21
Milk traffic, 35, 65, 69, 84, 97, 162
Moguls, 16, 90, 90, 109, 136, 169-70, 172, 178

Narrow gauge, 16, 165, 170, 172-4, 176
Nationalisation, 9, 13, 16, 20-1, 82, 89, 100, 116, 129-30, 132, 152, 169; anti-, 100
Neath & Brecon Railway, 186

Newcastle, 130, 132-4, 133, 152; – Swansea, 132
Newport, 23, 185
'Newspaper trains', 113
Non-stop runs, 22-3, 70, 109, 112, 114, 116-17, 129, 130, 132, 133, 145, 168
Norfolkman, 67
Norseman, 132
North British Railway, 148, 149, 152, 156
North Briton, 132
North Devon & Cornwall Junction Railway (Withered Arm), 51, 56, 56, 59-61
North East Region, 100, 129-34, 152
North Eastern Railway, 94, 129, 130, 147
North Warwickshire line, 99
Northern Counties Committee, 169, 172, 174, 177, 178
Northumbrian, 132
Nuneaton, 124, 190

Oban, 140, 149, 152, 156
Observation cars, 152
Outings, school, 38-40, 39, 41, 72
Overnight services, 32, 34, 35, 116, 133, 134, 152, 156 see also Sleepers
Oxford, 116, 183

Pacific 4-6-2s, 24, 57, 60-1, 83, 89, 90, 100; Battle of Britain class, 61, Squadron, 57, 58, Lord Beaverbrook, 73; Britannia class, 24, 89, 101, Lord Hurcomb, 67, Iron Duke, 59, William Shakespeare, 8; Class 7 Shooting Star, 20; Coronation class, 124, Princess, 128, Princess Margaret Rose, 78, Duchess of Montrose, 158; Duchess class, 89; Gresley A1 St Simon, 95, A2 A.H. Peppercorn, 143, A3 Flying Scotsman, 97, Tranquil, 98, White Knight, 131, A4, 24, 96-7, 100, 128, 133, 152, Kingfisher, 68, Mallard, 93, 98, 145, Miles Beevor, 12, Quicksilver, 150-1, Woodcock, 12; Merchant Navy class 60, 61, Blue Funnel, 61, Blue Star, 17, Cunard White Star, 58; Princess Royal class, Lady Patricia, 138; West Country class, 61, 75, City of Wells, 58, Combe Martin, 54-5, Dorchester, 62, Salisbury, 62
Paddington, 20, 23-6, passim, 28, 30, 31, 65, 74, 86, 88, 110, 179, 180, 183; – Birkenhead, 89; – Bristol, 26, 179; – Penzance, 25, 25; – Plymouth, 25, 113, 117; – St Ives, 105-14
Paignton, 37, 112, 132
Pannier tanks, 2, 15, 27, 28, 119
Patriot 4-6-0s, 7; Derbyshire Yeomanry, 2, 14; Royal Pioneer Corps, 7
Peak class 45 1Co-Co1, 104
Peak District, 82, 164-6, 181, 183
Penzance, 12, 25, 116
Peppercorn A1 Osprey, 150-1
Perth, 69, 152, 156, 189
Peterborough, 10, 127-8; – Yarmouth, 104
Peters, Ivo, 53, 120
Piloting, 13, 42, 119, 136, 144
Plymouth, 25, 109, 117, 149
Posters, 66, 78-9, 97, 97
Prairie tanks, 16, 28, 28, 110, 112, 114, 114, 135, 136, 162
Precursor 4-4-0 Tamerlane, 147
Preston, 69, 82, 120, 181
Prince of Wales 4-6-0 Queen of the Belgians, 89
Pull-and-push services, 81, 163
Pullmans, 13, 17, 22, 53, 61, 61, 62, 73, 83, 132, 134, 140; Queen of Scots, 132; Sunday, 132; Tees-Tyne, 93, 132, 150-1; Yorkshire, 132
Pwllheli, 119, 120

2-6-0 Queen Elizabeth, 175

Railcars, 168, 170, 176, 178
Railway Magazine, 24, 67
Raven, Sir Vincent, 147
Reading, 23, 108, 184
Red Dragon, 20; Rose, 123

Refreshment rooms, 65-7 passim, 69, 70, 72, 89, 153
Restaurant cars, 20, 22, 34, 38, 70, 76, 101, 115, 119, 125, 132, 138-41, 139, 149, 157, 173, 180, 181
Robinson, J.G., 145
Rolt, L.T.C., 172
Royal Duchy, 25, 25, 26, 101; Highlander, 187, 188; Scot, 123; Scot class, 78, 81, Queen's Westminster Rifleman, 77
Rubery, 15
Rugeley, 122, 123, 125-6; – Stourport, 87
Runaways, 164, 166, 176, 178
'Runners', 70

Safety, 27, 92, see also Accidents
Saint Mungo, 189
Saturday traffic, 12, 14, 60, 72, 74, 105, 114-20, 117, 132, 137, 157, 168
Scarborough, 97, 116, 120, 129, 132-4 passim; Flyer, 132
School 4-4-0s, 63; Charterhouse, 63; Clifton, 60
School trains, 40-1, 72
Scotland, 34-6 passim, 78, 79, 83, 94, 142-56; Region, 100, 152, 190
Sea Wall, 30, 105, 113
Selby, John, 43
Settle & Carlisle Railway (Long Drag), 83, 181, 183
Shamrock, 123
Sheds/Depots, 62, 81, 128, 162; Ballinamore, 174, 176; Barrow Road, Bristol, 7; Basingstoke, 62; Bushbury, 9; Exmouth Junction, 59; Gateshead, 98; Glanmire Road, Cork, 171; Laira 109; Middleton Top, 167; Monument Lane, Birmingham, 32, 47, 49; Neasden, 100, 146; Newton Abbot, 163; Nine Elms, 58; Pennyburn, Londonderry, 177, 177; Stafford, 123; Stewarts Lane, Battersea, 8, 59, 59; St Ives, 114; St Margarets, Edinburgh, 154-5; Weybridge, 61
Sheffield, 69, 94, 116, 126
Ships, 12, 60, 78, 169
Shrewsbury, 4, 88-9, 89, 121, 184, 185
Shunting, 13, 28, 46, 48, 61, 69, 70, 82, 89, 118, 123, 130, 134, 153, 153, 167, 183, 186
Silver Jubilee, 20, 70, 97
Single lines, 29, 47, 115, 149, 172, 186
Signals, 13, 13, 15, 27, 34, 43, 56, 69, 70, 82, 88, 118, 122, 124-6, 125, 130, 131, 134-7; bells, 36, 65, 66; boxes, 17, 34, 56, 66, 117, 123, 133, 135, 137
Sleepers, 34, 86, 116, 132, 133, 152, 156, 183, 187, 188, 190
Sligo, Leitrim & Northern Counties Railways, 170, 173
Somerset & Dorset Railway, 53, 54-5, 81, 116, 120, 126
South Eastern & Chatham Railway, 56
South Yorkshireman, 132
Southampton, 60, 120, 182, 183
Southern Railway, 24, 25, 53-63, 140
Specials, 32, 34, 37, 60, 72, 81, 91, 126, 166, 166, 177; banana, 84; cattle, 162; educational, 37, 39, 39, 104; hop pickers, 60, 161; postal, 32; Starlight, 116, 152; sporting, 37, 72, football, 37, 85-6, racing, 37, 86; VIPs, 53
Speed, 13, 23, 24, 60, 86, 97, 100, 108, 109, 119, 136, 174
Sprinters, 23
Stamp, Lord, 80, 81
Stanier, Sir William, 80, 81, 188
Starcross, 105, 106-7
Stations, 9, 13, 31, 64-74, 77, 78, 81; staff, 24, 26, 68-9, 85, 88-9, 93-4, 130
Steamers, paddle, 104, 143, 148; Lincoln Castle, 101
St Erth, 111, 114
St Ives, 110, 114, 114
Stockton & Darlington Railway, 130
St Pancras, 20, 79, 82, 83; – Edinburgh, 132, 180, 181; – Glasgow, 12, 152, 181; – Manchester, 12, 83, 181, 183

Strabane, 176, 177
Stranorlar, 176, 177
Stranraer, 132, 152
Sugar beet traffic, 93-4, 97, 100, 161
Summits, Masbury, 186; Shap, 138, 142, 181; Whiteball, 39
Sunday services, 34, 60, 86, 115, 120
Swansea, 132, 184, 186; – Penzance, 25
Swindon, 23, 30, 33, 132, 179; – Bristol, 84

Tailte 4-6-0, 170
Talisman, 132
Teignmouth, 9, 105, 113
'Terrier' tank, 52
Thanet/Kentish Belle, 73
Thompson, Edward, 154
Through the Window, 109
Tickets, 173; Circular, 184, 186; excess, 181; platform, 67-8; Regulation, 119, Runabout, 116, 120, 132, 156, 156; season, 45
Timetables, 24, 96, 115-18, 132, 141, 143, 156, 173, 190; ABC, 180; Bradshaw, 115
Token exchangers, 13, 16, 135-7 passim
Track, 30, 78, 83, 86, 100
Tralee & Dingle Railway, 168, 170, 173-4
Trams, 142, 169
Treacy, Bishop, 100
Trent Valley line, 122-8, 122, 124
Tunnels, 42, 105, 164; Mountfield, 60; Mutley, 109; Parsons, 9, 30; Penge, 57; Pennine, 183; Severn, 185; Whiteball, 109
Turntables, 45-7 passim
Tynesider, 132

Ulster, 80, 152, 169, 172, 176-8; Transport Authority, 172, 178
Uppingham, 13

Valentia Harbour branch, 173
Valve gear, 64, 89, 94
Veltom, Oliver, 88
Viaducts, Dawlish, 105; Dowery Dell, 14; Langston, 53; Largin, 29; Owencarrow, 177; St Germans, 112
Victoria, 22, 61, 73; – Dover, 22

Waiting rooms, 36, 46, 48, 65, 66, 69, 72
Wales, Central, 90, 185, 185; North, 79, 82, 94, 120; South, 28, 78, 185, – Paddington, 20, 23, 24; see also Cambrian
Walker, Sir Herbert, 56-7
Warship diesels, 2, 28, 29, 29, 41
Watering, 10-11, 85, 86-7, 116, 144, 147, 168, 174, 178; troughs, 60, 86, 147
Waterloo, 53, 56, 63, 120, 183; – Bournemouth, 17; – Lymington Pier, 63
Waverley, 132, 152, 180, 181
Weather, 35-6, 59, 157; floods, 87, 132; fog, 32, 162-3; snow, 36-7, 87, fences, 142
Wells, 81
Welshpool, 88, 90, 90
Wenford Bridge line, 56, 61
West Clare Railway, 172, 174, 178
West Coast main line, 79, 79, 83, 152, 180, 183
West Highland Railway, 152-3, 156
West Riding Limited, 20, 132
Western Region, 9, 13, 25-31, 74, 105-14, 162, 164
Weymouth, 30, 61; – Swindon, 33
Whale, George, 147
Whisky traffic, 35, 133
White Rose, 12, 132
Wolverhampton, 4, 9, 12, 25, 89, 127
Works, 86, 96; Cowlairs, 156; Swindon, 31, 41, 41, 127
World War I, 19, 187; II, 9, 12, 16, 20, 32, 60, 100, 169

Yards, freight, 35, 42, 46, 48, 93, 123, 135, 160-1; marshalling, 12, 137, 157, 162, Washwood Heath, 159
Yarmouth, 104, 184
York, 69, 74, 104, 104, 117, 120, 129, 130, 134, 152, 181